Thunder on the Right

Understanding Conservative Christianity

Elizabeth C. Nordbeck

A Kaleidoscope Series Resource

United Church Press
New York

For Paul
Who helps me persevere

KALEIDOSCOPE SERIES

Library of Congress Cataloging-in-Publication Data

Nordbeck, Elizabeth.
    Thunder on the right : understanding conservative Christianity /
Elizabeth Nordbeck. — Leader's guide ed.
        p.   cm. — (A Kaleidoscope series resource)
    Includes bibliographical references.
    ISBN 0-8298-0820-5
    1. Fundamentalism—Study and teaching.   2. Evangelicalism—Study
and teaching.   3. Pentecostalism—Study and teaching.   4. United
States—Church history—20th century—Study and teaching.
    I.   Title.   II.   Series.
BT82.2.N67   1990
270.8'2—dc20   90-34413

United Church Press, 475 Riverside Drive, New York, NY 10115

Contents

How to Use the Kaleidoscope Series

The Kaleidoscope book is the basic resource in the Kaleidoscope Series. For each Kaleidoscope book there is a Leader's Guide edition, which has a sixteen-page Leader's Guide bound into the back of the book. The leader will need to study both the text and the Leader's Guide to prepare to lead study sessions of the Kaleidoscope Series resources. The video is a very helpful tool for the leader and the group when using this book as a study resource.

Introduction to the Kaleidoscope Series

Through direct experience, our faculty at Lancaster Theological Seminary discovered that a continual demand exists for Christian theological reflection upon issues of current interest. To meet this demand, the Seminary for many years has offered courses for lay people. To offer the substance of these courses to the wider Christian public is the purpose of the Kaleidoscope Series.

Lancaster Seminary exists to proclaim the gospel of Jesus Christ for the sake of the church and the world. In addition to preparing men and women for the ordained Christian ministry, the Seminary seeks to be a center of theological reflection for clergy and laity. Continuing education and leadership development for all Christians focus our mission. The topics and educational style in the Kaleidoscope Series extend Lancaster Seminary's commitment: theological study reflective of the interaction of the Bible, the world, the church, worship, and personal faith. We hope that this course will provide an opportunity for you to grow in self-understanding, in knowledge of other people and God's creation, and in the spirit of Christ.

We wish to thank the staff of the Division of Education and Publication of the United Church Board for Homeland Ministries for their leadership in this enterprise. The Rev. Dr. Ansley Coe Throckmorton, The Rev. Dr. Larry E. Kalp, and The Rev. Dr.

Percel O. Alston provided encouragement and support for the project. In particular, we are grateful for the inspiration of Percel Alston, who was a trustee of Lancaster Seminary. His life-long interest in adult education makes it most appropriate that this series be dedicated to him. Three other staff members have guided the series through the writing and production stages: The Rev. Jack H. Haney, Project Coordinator for the Kaleidoscope Series, The Rev. Nancy G. Wright, Editor for Kaleidoscope, and Mr. Gene Permé, Marketing Director. As a publishing staff they have provided valuable experience and counsel. Finally, I wish to recognize the creative leadership of Mrs. Jean Vieth, the Seminary Coordinator for the Series who has been active for several years in this educational program at Lancaster.

Peter M. Schmiechen, President
The Lancaster Theological Seminary

Preface

Several years ago I was asked to design and lead a two-day, continuing education event at Lancaster Theological Seminary in Pennsylvania. The class, entitled "Thunder on the Right: Understanding Conservative Christianity," proved so popular that it was subsequently expanded into an equally popular evening course and opened to the general public in the Lancaster area. Somewhat to my surprise, the men and women who participated were not doctrinaire liberals, looking for theological ammunition with which to combat "fundamentalism" (a word often used generically, if incorrectly, to describe conservative Christianity). To be sure, mainline churchgoers did dominate the groups. But there were also self-professed evangelicals from a wide variety of backgrounds, including Mennonites, Brethren, Reformed, and Independents, as well as mainline and independent charismatics.

The groups shared mutual misunderstandings. Several evangelical participants, for instance, were startled to discover that their fellow mainline students actually had real spiritual depth, and they were amazed at the seriousness with which the latter approached theology. Liberals, in turn, were surprised at both the variety of theological positions found among conservatives and the sophistication with which these were discussed. Virtually everyone came with a similar learning goal: to understand more about the beliefs of others with whom they—sometimes without knowing exactly why—did not agree and, in so doing, to understand more about their own beliefs. The basic purpose of this book is the same:

to help its readers acknowledge and articulate their own theological views and to engender understanding of (though not necessarily agreement with) views that seem to differ. It is intended as a nontechnical, brief introduction to a fairly complex subject. Interested readers will, it is to be hoped, continue their studies in the large and growing corpus of scholarly works on the topic of evangelical Christianity.

As a pastor and professor in the United Church of Christ, I have written with an unavoidably liberal bias, which will surely be evident in many ways, both subtle and obvious. Nevertheless, the intent of the volume is descriptive, not polemical or apologetic. I have outlined as neutrally and accurately as possible conservative positions on a variety of topics and compared them to mainline positions, for the most part without evaluative discussion. In one sense, of course, this is a nearly impossible task, because both mainline and conservative Christianity are extremely diverse phenomena. Any generalization is a distortion at some level, and undoubtedly there are representatives of both groups whose viewpoints I have here oversimplified or ignored. Nevertheless, consistent themes characterize these two diverse groups, and it is on these I have sought to focus.

The final chapter is an exception to the general policy of nonjudgmental reporting. In it I have attempted to answer the question "What can these groups teach each other in their common effort to be faithful to the gospel?"

One final note: For some people, the most pressing issue is not "What do conservative Christians believe?" but "Why is conservative Christianity so popular?" The growth of conservative Christianity has been explained variously by historians as a by-product of democratic individualism and demographics; by psychologists as a manifestation of high personal authority needs; by sociologists as a function of social dislocation and deprivation; by economists as a residue of class struggle; by conservative theologians as visible evidence of America's God-given high destiny and calling—and fair warning about the consequences of ignoring them; by liberal interpreters as a function of arrested growth in an early stage of faith development. Perhaps Jesus' own words are here as significant as any: "The wind blows where it wills, and you hear the sound of it, but you do not know whence it comes or whither it

goes; so it is with everyone who is born of the Spirit [John 3:8]."
This volume, in any case, makes no attempt to answer the why
question. Its concern is largely theological: What do conservative
Christians believe about the individual Christian, the church, the
wider society? How do these beliefs compare with those that
characterize the Protestant mainline?

Introduction

"Our government," said Dwight D. Eisenhower in the mid-1950s, "makes no sense unless it is founded on a deeply felt religious faith—and I don't care what faith it is." Articulating the social and moral value of what might be called generic religion, Eisenhower reflected the bland and broad religious ethos of postwar America. But as the twentieth century draws to a close, many Americans—a vocal minority that some have estimated to be forty million or more strong—would consider Eisenhower's remark nothing short of heresy. These are conservative Christians, or, as they are frequently called, born-again Christians or evangelicals. And their phenomenal rise in influence, power, and visibility since 1970 has led observers to dub the last quarter of this century the "evangelical awakening."[1]

Like the first great religious awakening that surprised colonial America during the decades from 1720 to 1770, erupting and subsiding in different locations and under different leadership, the recent evangelical resurgence has been both surprising and socially significant. Between the 1976 election of Jimmy Carter, who was reported to have won despite his strong evangelical connections, and the election of Ronald Reagan, who, many claimed, won because of his evangelical connections, America's so-called silent religious majority decisively found their public voices. And the heritage many of these believers claimed was not, as Dwight Eisenhower might have wished, that of citizens merely of a religious America, but of a specifically Christian America.

xiii

The rise of what has variously been called the new "evangelicalism," "new evangelical united front," and "new Christian right" is not only evident in presidential politics. Christian schools—sectarian alternatives to grades kindergarten through twelve—are thriving, as are the more traditional Bible colleges and seminaries. Evangelical scholars, centered in nationally accredited schools like Wheaton College in Illinois or Gordon-Conwell and Fuller Theological Seminaries, are respected and in demand professionally. Despite several much-publicized personal scandals during the late 1980s, Christian radio and television stations have become a significant presence in a broadcasting environment that only a few years ago scheduled religious programming in the "dead time," Sunday mornings and after midnight. Political action groups with names like Christian Voice, Conservative Caucus, Pro-Family Coalition, and Intercessors for America seek aggressively to influence secular decision makers.

If it is clear that America is presently in a period of heightened evangelical religious activity, it is considerably less clear who these "new" believers are, where they have come from, what they believe, and what their relationship might be to other branches of Christendom. Although a good deal of excellent self-critical, scholarly work has been done within the last two decades by conservative scholars, relatively little that is not of a polemical nature has been written to interpret the movement to non-evangelicals. The present volume is an attempt to examine the above questions briefly and to provide an accessible introduction for those persons outside the movement who would like to understand more about conservative Christianity.

To do this is not a simple task. Part of the difficulty in understanding the conservative phenomenon derives from the vastness and historic complexity of the movement itself. Although outsiders often perceive conservative Christianity as a twentieth-century monolith, diverse in its forms but united at its core, the movement is far from that. Historical, doctrinal, theological, ecclesiological, organizational, and liturgical differences abound. And, unlike the liberal, or mainline, Protestant churches,[2] in which tolerance for theological differences is the norm, many conservative Christians understand such variations as marking the boundaries between those who are saved and those who are not.

Like any other large bloc, moreover, conservative Christianity has its own extreme "fringe" groups. Because of the distinctiveness or peculiarity of their beliefs, they are significantly different from the majority of conservatives yet resemble them more than they do any other group. Appalachian snake handlers, unitarian or "oneness" pentecostals, and radical fundamentalists who would reinstate Mosaic law fall into this category. And because the fringe groups regularly receive greater media attention than the others, it is often these groups that serve to define conservative Christianity, however inaccurately, for mainline Christians and other observers.

Even giving a generally acceptable name to conservative believers is difficult. Typically, scholars have attached the label "evangelical" to conservatives, but this term is potentially confusing and inaccurate. Both fundamentalists and evangelicals—two subcultures within the broader category of evangelicals—take pains to distinguish thmselves from each other because of what they understand to be their significant theological differences. Well-known moderate fundamentalist leader Jerry Falwell, for instance, has criticized the bankruptcy of contemporary evangelicalism because of its overtolerance of theological pluralism. Evangelicals, for their part, frequently prefer to dissociate themselves from the narrow-minded legalism and literalism they believe have characterized much fundamentalism. Members of both groups may find the distinctive beliefs and practices of charismatics or pentecostals theologically unacceptable.

The umbrella term *evangelical* is problematic for another reason. Within mainline Protestantism, many Christians are reluctant to give over a richly evocative, historic label to one particular segment of contemporary Christendom. They point out that *evangelical*—derived from the Greek work *euangelion,* meaning good news or gospel—was used in the early church simply to designate believers in Christ's saving birth, death, and resurrection. Throughout the nineteenth century, *evangelical* described virtually all the mainline American denominations, including Episcopalians. At least one mainline group, the product of a recent merger of three Lutheran bodies, has deliberately claimed its historic heritage in a new name, the Evangelical Lutheran Church in America. For all these reasons, the generic term *conservative Christianity,* despite its unfortunate political overtones, seems pref-

erable. Conservative Christians by no means agree on the nature
of the true gospel of Jesus Christ. But virtually all of them do seek
in various ways to conserve that divine message as they understand
it, to uphold its purity, and to protect it from what they see as the
subversive encroachments of human beings. While liberals for the
past century have enthusiastically and sometimes uncritically embraced new theologies, new interpretive tools, and new biblical
interpretations, conservatives respond to these innovations with
anything from caution to outright hostility. Deeply aware of the
sovereignty of God and the limitations of humankind, conservative
Christians seek to follow a gospel that is in its essence simple,
personally accessible, and without need of alterations from modern
society, ecclesiastical structures, or academic scholarship.

Chapter 1

Who Are the
Conservative Christians?

Conservative Christians, writes one commentator, "are a grouping for which no one party could choose to speak."[1] They are
linked by no single organization, council, or bureaucracy. Indeed,
historically, conservatives have often been separatistic, dis-
putatious, and mutually hostile. Yet undeniably, they share a strong
family resemblance that cuts across denominational and even deep
theological boundaries. Or to put it differently: conservative
Christians, in all their diversity, are far more like one another than
they are like mainline Protestants or other Christian bodies.

What is the nature of this family resemblance that links evangelicals and fundamentalists, charismatics and pentecostals?
Church historian Grant Wacker offers an economical definition of
evangelicalism that provides a clue. Evangelicals, writes Wacker,
believe "the sole authority in religion is the Bible and the sole
means of salvation is a life-transforming experience wrought by the
Holy Spirit through Faith in Jesus Christ."[2] This definition, while
it leaves much unsaid, suggests that conservative Christians are
united in their concern for two supremely important matters. The
first of these is doctrine, the concrete, essential beliefs that
Christians hold about their faith. The second is equally important
but more elusive. It is a changed or transformed life, which
necessarily issues in characteristic attitudes or habits of the mind
and heart. It is these habits and attitudes, in particular, that
influence the ways in which doctrine is actually received. Understanding conservative Christianity, then, involves looking first at

1

the major doctrines that believers share, and second, at the emphases and themes that provide the interpretive lenses through which doctrine is perceived.

Basic Doctrines

Although theological differences can easily be chronicled, most conservative Christians hold tenaciously to several basic doctrines of orthodox Protestantism. These doctrines are neither new nor unique to conservatives. They are, in fact, to be discovered in the historic creeds, platforms, and statements of faith held by most Protestant Christians worldwide.

The Inspiration of the Holy Scriptures

This is perhaps the single most basic affirmation that conservatives share. The Bible is not merely a conglomeration of legends, stories, and folk tales, interspersed with historical facts. Rather, it is the true record of God's creative and gracious acts in history. Conservatives differ greatly in their understanding of the nature of God's "authorship" or participation in the writing of the Bible, and in the weight and veracity they give to its different parts. But they are agreed that the Bible is, in some real sense, truly God's eternal word and not merely the time-bound, self-absorbed words of human beings, however exemplary or devout. And this means that the Bible is of central importance in a believer's life.

The Trinity

With the exception of a few "oneness," or unitarian, pentecostals, conservatives are united in their acceptance of the foundational Christian doctrine of the Trinity. The Nicene Creed, affirmed by the church in A.D. 451, reads: "We believe in one God, the Father, the Almighty. . . . We believe in one Lord, Jesus Christ, the only Son of God. . . . We believe in the Holy Spirit, the Lord, the giver of life."[3] Although God is truly one being, God is revealed to humanity in three coequal and coeternal persons, or manifestations: as sovereign and judging Creator, as saving and suffering Christ, as comforting and sustaining Spirit. Occasionally, conservatives do fall into what has been called an "unconscious unitarianism" of the second or third person of the Trinity. In their prayer or worship lives they may, for example, emphasize the friendship of Jesus or the ministrations and gifts of the Holy Spirit. But most are insistent on the theological importance of trinitarian doctrine and language.

The Depravity of Humankind

The term *depravity* used in this context does not imply that all human beings are wholly evil. Rather depravity indicates that every man and woman has a natural bias of the heart, or predilection, toward sin and selfishness. This bias, like an insidious cancer untreated, keeps persons from true spiritual health and separates them from God and one another. Nor can they overcome this deadly liability by good works and acts of will. Only through God's grace, freely given, can human natures be turned around toward the good, and human behavior come to reflect that inward change.

The Incarnation of the Divine Christ

Because of God's great love for the fallen world, God actually chose to become human. The incarnation (or "enfleshing") marks the entrance of the divine and eternal into history in the form of a person, Jesus Christ, who participated fully in all the pain and humiliation of humanness. Jesus was more than an exemplary human being, more than a person with divine attributes, more than a kind of demigod. He was fully human and fully God at one and the same time. Many conservatives have a relatively high Christology, or doctrine of Christ, which in practice emphasizes the divine Christ, his sonship and sacrifice, to a greater degree than it does the human Jesus and his teachings.

The Atonement and Resurrection

When humankind first lapsed from grace by disobeying God, the result was death and alienation: "the wages of sin is death [Rom. 6:23]." But God, still loving the fallen creation, at the appropriate time offered Jesus to serve as a sacrifice, literally a payment, for human sins. Jesus' crucifixion was that payment. In dying, Jesus gave his own sinless life as an atoning, or expiating substitute, for our sinful ones; thereafter, every person who believes in him "should not perish but have eternal life [John 3:16]." Jesus' resurrection—his actual, physical mastery of the finality and decay of death—is the central fact of the New Testament church. Because Jesus was raised from the dead, people can believe in the truth of his message about God's love, and they can have hope about their own eternal futures.

Conversion

Conversion (from a Latin root that means "to turn") signifies the turning away from our former sinful natures toward God. Because every man, woman, and child is tainted with sin, no one is exempt from the need for conversion. Conservative Christians admit that conversion experiences will often be quite different for different people. One person may have a single cataclysmic encounter with God, much as Paul did on the road to Damascus, while another may have a series of spiritual experiences that lead finally to a personal "decision for Christ." Yet virtually all conservatives would agree that some moment of conscious choice or crisis is necessary, an identifiable time of repentance and commitment after which one may say truthfully, "I once was lost but now am found." This is seen as the moment of regeneration, when God through grace frees women and men from the sinful bias of their hearts and offers them both new hearts and new lives.

But the process of conversion doesn't end there. The change in a person's inner self eventually manifests itself in outward behavior that models a faithful Christian life-style. Conservatives have markedly different opinions about the extent to which Christian perfection in this life is possible and even about the meaning of the phrase "a faithful life-style." But they are in agreement that a person must become a new person in Christ and that this internal and invisible change must be reflected outwardly and visibly.

Christ's Return and Final Judgment

Probably no single doctrine is more controversial or divisive— within the extended fellowship of conservatives and without—than that of Christ's Second Coming. While many mainline Protestants deal with this doctrine largely by ignoring it, conservatives take it most seriously. Particularly among fundamentalists, the doctrine provides the context for the examination of both personal piety and social policy. But important questions remain problematic: What is the precise relationship between the Second Coming and the thousand-year reign of righteousness described in the Book of Revelation? What is the relationship between Christ's return and the time of tribulation, during which evil will hold sway and the antichrist will appear? How close at hand are all these events? What is clear to most conservatives is that human history *will* come to a decisive end. Thus it is important for persons to be spiritually prepared. Christ will surely return to judge all human beings, living and dead; and believers and unbelievers will be separated for eternity into realms of joy and punishment.

Both conservative and mainline Christians reading the basic doctrines above may be startled to learn that they share with their brothers and sisters a core of beliefs on which they can conscientiously agree. Why, then, is there such divisiveness between these groups? The answer is that many, perhaps most, of the differences between conservative and liberal Christians have to do not with differing doctrinal statements but with the way in which such statements are understood, interpreted, and acted upon. To assess all the historical, cultural, and theological reasons for these differences is beyond the scope of this book. It is evident, however, that conservatives share a number of distinctive perspectives, or ways of looking at the world, that provide the characteristic filters through which they perceive and interpret doctrine. And these perspectives are very different from those of mainline Protestantism.[4] Six areas of difference may be identified:

Attitude Toward Pluralism

In general, mainline Protestant churches accept into their fold persons holding a wide range of interpretations of the doctrinal stands described above. In the liberal United Church of Christ, for example, a representative congregational statement of faith reads: "Our fellowship is not dependent upon identity of theological opinion, but upon a common loyalty to Jesus, and a common passion to do justice, to love kindness, and to walk humbly with our God."[5] Although doctrinal boundaries do exist, diversity of interpretation is acceptable within a broad and pluralistic fellowship; and, indeed, pluralism is often celebrated as a gracious gift of God. Among conservatives there is a much narrower range of acceptable interpretations. Pluralism, far from being productive and stimulating of theological inquiry, is more likely to be understood by them as potentially dangerous and seductive of truth.

The Importance of Doctrinal Standards

In mainline churches individuals may hold widely variant views about, for example, Christ's second coming or the role of Mary, Jesus' mother. In conservative churches, however, it is important that the particular content of belief be correct; specific doctrinal understandings matter, not simply to church leaders, but to God. To insist on purity of doctrinal standards is not to be arbitrary, legalistic, or rigid. Rather it is to uphold the purity of the biblical faith, without which Christianity is meaningless. Conservatives believe there is a direct relationship between what one believes and who one is, between who one is and what one does. Therefore, it is important to maintain purity of belief so that one may truly be a Christian. While liberal Protestants (contrary to the suspicions of some conservative critics) by no means ignore doctrinal matters, they are far more likely to regard doctrinal specifics as nonessential to Christian personhood, and to sever the link between particularity of belief and "being Christian." Thus for liberals it is often deemed more important that one seek, with the help of the Holy Spirit, to follow Jesus, than to articulate precisely who Jesus is. Or to use a different example: a majority of liberal Protestants do believe in the virgin birth of Christ, but many of them will contend that this belief is not essential to their faith in Christ's saving power. Conservatives, however, argue that without belief in a literal virgin birth, essentials of the faith are endangered, and, more important, an unbeliever's soul may be at risk.

Emphasis on Boundaries and Dichotomies

Conservatives are inclined to see the contours of reality in clear, black and white relief more often than are liberal Protestants. Reality consists of various alternatives, or pairs of opposites—good and evil, heaven and hell, saved and unsaved—and these opposites are on the whole clear and easily discernible to conservatives. These opposites present men and women with choices, the proper answers to which are usually evident (although the human will to answer properly is not always so easily summoned). Conservatives tend to be boundary makers and keepers: personally, doctrinally, and denominationally it is important to be clear about what separates "us" from "others." And for fundamentalists who take literally the biblical mandate to be separate, it is important to ensure that these boundaries remain high and impregnable. Thus institutional separatism and independence are characteristic of many conservatives (though by no means all), while cooperation and ecumenism more often characterize the Protestant mainline. On the whole, liberals are more likely to see reality in various shades of gray; to see choice making as situational and complex, rather than simple and absolute; and to understand boundaries as important but not inviolable.

Individualism

At the center of the church is the individual believer. Great variation exists among conservatives concerning the role, if any, of social action and outreach in the churches. But remarkable consensus is found in the idea that real change can happen only after women and men have been changed from within, through God's grace. A concern for individual conversion as the necessary prerequisite for effective outreach links conservative Christianity with some of its most familiar characteristics: interest in revivalism and high visibility television programming; emphasis on soul saving; concern for healing and wholeness ministries; and comparative disinterest in solving what liberal Protestants refer to as "systemic" social problems, such as economic inequality and the destruction of the environment.

Emphasis on Evangelism

To spread the evangel—the good news about Christ—is important to all Christians. Yet conservatives, far more than liberal Protestants or other Christian groups, rank evangelism as a central, perhaps the central, outreach task of the churches. Publishing, teaching, foreign and domestic missions, personal witnessing—all these are intended to "tell the old, old story" directly and intentionally. Although mainline Protestantism as a whole is increasingly concerned about evangelism, its representatives are far more likely to do their witnessing indirectly and obliquely, through service and action rather than direct teaching, confronting, or proselytizing. And while mainline Christians affirm service ministries as ends in themselves, conservatives more often regard them as means to the more important end of winning new converts.

Emphasis on Religious Experience

Since the Great Awakening of the 1740s, evangelical religion has been popularly associated with emotionalism and anti-intellectualism. Today more than a few conservatives remain suspicious of higher education as subversive of true piety and participate in worship experiences that are characterized by heightened or extreme emotion. The majority of conservatives, however, support education—though not necessarily of the liberal arts variety—and enjoy worship that is warmly affective witout being highly emotional. What unites this broad spectrum of believers is a common emphasis on the importance of religious "experience," on faith that is apprehended both through the intellect and the feelings, or heart. Many would agree with Jonathan Edwards and John Wesley that a believer whose heart is not "strangely warmed" or who is "destitute of pious affections" is probably not a believer at all. Indeed, they argue, how could a genuinely transforming encounter with the living God fail to elicit extremely strong human feelings and emotions? Mainline Christians, on the other hand, maintain that the elevation of experience as a sine qua non of the religious life can result all too easily in a high level of religious subjectivity and the subordination of sound doctrine and practice.

During the 1980s both conservative and liberal Christians have moved intentionally toward a more wholistic understanding of their faith. A new emphasis on spirituality within the mainline has led to greater concern for religious experience, while the quest for intellectual respectability has impelled conservatives to promote more rigorous standards for education and scholarship. Nevertheless, experience rather than intellectual understanding remains the most critical datum for many conservatives.

Who are the people who share these various doctrines and emphases, and where have they come from? Interpreters of contemporary religion identify anywhere from three to a dozen types,

or categories, within the conservative spectrum. We will consider
five distinct groups: fundamentalists, pentecostals, new evangelicals, historic evangelicals, and charismatics. But it is extremely
important to recognize that none of these groups is anything like a
pure type, bounded by hard and fast divisions. Moreover, although
it is possible to generalize by contrasting conservative with mainline or liberal Christianity, there are millions of self-professed
evangelicals and charismatics within the mainline denominations
themselves.[6] Virtually all of these denominations have formally
organized evangelical and charismatic fellowships, which typically
understand their function to be renewal, or "leaven," for the
whole.

Despite the surprise with which the "new" evangelicalism has
been greeted, the roots of conservative Christianity reach all the
way back to the Protestant Reformation of the sixteenth century,
when vocal critics like Martin Luther, Ulrich Zwingli, and John
Calvin broke with the Roman Catholic church because of the
corruptions they perceived in it. These and other reformers criticized the church for elevating its historic practices and teachings
above the scriptures as the measure of true faith. They were
convinced that the Bible alone—*sola scriptura*—provides an adequate and timeless measure for faith and practice; any other
authority represents a departure from historical Christianity. Similarly, the reformers challenged the prevailing assumption that
righteousness could be bought through personal deeds and acts of
penance mediated by the church. Grace alone—*sola gratia*—freely
offered by God to individual persons is the Christian's hope, not
acts of human will or institutional mediation. One important result
of the Reformation, then, was a new understanding of God's
essential accessibility to ordinary men and women through the
scriptures and through personal experiences of grace.

These and other insights of the reformers were summarized in
the Westminster Confession of 1647, which with some modifications remains today an important standard for interpreting biblical
teachings and a source for conservative doctrine. At its center is a
thoroughgoing belief in the sovereignty of God and the utter
helplessness and dependency of sinful humanity.

The late Sydney Ahlstrom has identified four important developments that emerged from these new convictions, initially trans-

lated to the New World through the experience of New England Puritanism. First was the "new kind of Christian piety that grew out of the anxieties produced by the doctrine of election," anxieties that made a doctrine of assurance of salvation "existentially central." Without the formal assurances of a mediating church, only a vital inward experience offered Puritans the concrete hope that they were among the redeemed. Second, the new emphasis on inward experience made clear the differences between saved and unsaved, and in time these differences were recognized institutionally, as church membership became dependent upon a person's ability to recount a distinct conversion experience. One result was "an enduring tendency to separatism and to controversies on the question of fellowship." Third, the desire for "specific, biblical warrant for all matters of both ethics and church order" led early to divisiveness and controversy over scriptural interpretation. And finally, the Puritans "developed a new set of attitudes toward the social order," an ethic that objected to profligacy and privilege while it encouraged personal enterprise and effort.[7]

In time, as with most movements, the zeal and fervency of the first generation of Puritans waned, their devotional practices hardened into formal observance, and their ministers lamented the sorry state of the churches. Beginning in the late 1720s, however—and encouraged during the next two decades by the preaching of men like Jonathan Edwards and George Whitefield—revival swept unexpectedly through the colonies. This Great Awakening was a resurgence of the older Puritan tradition, a return to the founders' insistence on an inward experience of regeneration. The Awakening, America's first real intercolonial movement, was revolutionary in several ways. Its emphasis on the primacy of religious experience led to a distrust of formal education and to a "come-outer" mentality, as men and women left their "dull and dead" churches to form so-called New Light congregations. And the Awakening encouraged cooperation among these believers, making revival an acceptable, if unpredictable, part of Christian life and ministry.

At the end of the eighteenth century, a second Awakening again rekindled the East Coast, this time extending into the opening frontier. It combined powerfully with a rising American social consciousness and postrevolutionary zeal for missions. With multiple concerns that ranged from Sunday schools to temperance, the resulting nineteenth-century "evangelical united front" constituted an informal, ecumenical coalition of the several major denominations that eventually became the Protestant mainline. Despite differences in polity, practice, and doctrine, common social concerns and a common heritage minimized denominational rivalries and antagonisms for the time being. The optimistic goal of many of these believers was the same: to help mold a "Christian America" of hardworking, pious women and men eager to do God's will—and perhaps even to assist as partners in the hastening of God's earthly kingdom.[8]

But this grand idealistic vision was short lived. By the close of the nineteenth century, revolutionary developments—civil war, industrial growth, urbanization, immigration, innovations in science and technology—combined to effect unimagined changes in the fabric of society. In the face of such massive upheaval and transformation, America's evangelical coalition fractured and factionalized. Thus the stage was set for the rise of a multivoiced alternative Protestant culture.

Subgroups of Conservative Christianity

Fundamentalists

Of the five subgroups of conservative Christianity, fundamentalism is perhaps the most readily identifiable. Often used indiscriminately by liberals to designate anyone significantly more conservative than they are, the term has a precise historical and contemporary meaning. George Marsden, foremost historian of American fundamentalism, describes members of the movement as "evangelical Christians, close to the traditions of the dominant American revivalist establishment of the nineteenth century, who in the twentieth century militantly opposed both modernism in theology and the cultural changes that modernism endorsed."[9]

To understand this fundamentalist impulse, it is necessary to understand what it was that fundamentalists were reacting against. At the end of the nineteenth century, Protestants responded to their environment in characteristically different ways. Some liberal, or progressive, Protestants developed what is generally called a modernist approach to social and scientific change, opting to assimilate new data into historic Christian positions. For example, challenged by Darwin's theories of evolution and natural selection, they concluded that biblical creation and evolution were not incompatible; evolution may be understood simply as God's way of accomplishing the divine purpose. Nor does this understanding undermine the truth and sacredness of the Bible, for the creation stories illustrate the essential truth that God was involved in every detail of the creation and now proclaims that it is good.

Four controversial affirmations underlay this emerging modernist thought. [10] First, liberals stressed the importance of inductive inquiry; that is, they demanded that religion, including biblical study, be subject to the same rigorous tests that people use to verify other areas of human knowledge. Second, liberalism tended to elevate human experience, understood in the broadest sense, above the scriptures as a source of religious authority. The Bible itself is authoritative not because it is divinely authored but because it presents a convincing record of human experience of the living God. Third, liberals emphasized the linkage between the human and the divine, between reason and revelation. Not only is God immanent, present in human affairs, but people learn about God and about themselves in the same ways: through observation, encounter, analysis. Finally, liberals expressed confidence in human ability and its power to overcome personal and social obstacles. Stressing humankind's potential for the good rather than its propensity for evil, liberals affirmed that men and women were called to be co-workers with God in eliminating social inequities and injustice.

But not all people responded to the changing times in the same optimistic way. Some Protestants, deeply troubled by what they believed to be the softening and undermining of historical Christian doctrines and truths, responded by emphatically rejecting all progressive and humanistic tendencies. At the turn of the century many of these conservatives remained restlessly in their denominations. But unlike their liberal counterparts, they continued to stress the supernatural origins of the "inerrant" scriptures and the essentially flawed nature of humanity.

Initially this new conservative bloc was quite diverse. It included theologically unsophisticated persons, as well as scholars like Princeton's brilliant J. Gresham Machen, who argued persuasively that there were certain essentials of the faith without which Christianity is merely a well-intentioned humanism. It also included supporters of revivals, many of whom had come to believe that God deals with humanity in distinct and differentiated eras, or "dispensations." This innovative historical scheme, called premillennial dispensationalism, was popularized by the famous annotated Scofield Reference Bible, published in 1909 and widely distributed thereafter. Dispensationalists rejected the optimism of both liberals and earlier evangelicals and taught the literal fulfillment of biblical prophecies that predict a period of apostasy and social disarray before Christ's imminent return.

By 1920, a broad coalition of fundamentalists—having now acquired a name borrowed from a series of pamphlets entitled *The Fundamentals for Today* (1910–15)—hoped to regain control of their denominations from liberal leaders. But their so-called antimodernist crusade was a bitter failure. Embarrassed by a highly publicized, humiliating defeat in the famous Scopes Monkey Trial at Dayton, Ohio, fundamentalists withdrew. Within two decades the movement had coalesced around an increasingly separatistic and militant core. Premillennial dispensationalism, formerly one strong element within the movement, became so widespread that it now virtually defined fundamentalism itself.[11]

With the conservative resurgence of the 1970s and after, fundamentalism has once again emerged into public prominence, but with some visible changes. Spokespersons like Jerry Falwell admit that today fundamentalism has "two basic contingents. One is the classic unbending militant group. The other is younger and more thoughtful," open to the possibility of change.[12] Although militancy, separatism, and dispensationalism remain hallmarks of the fundamentalist position, some scholars differentiate between "open" fundamentalists, who are willing to interact minimally with nonfundamentalists, and "separatist" fundamentalists, who resolutely resist any contact with groups tainted by modernism.

New Evangelicals and Historic Evangelicals

With the narrowing of the fundamentalist coalition, conservative Protestants who did not identify with militant separatism or dispensationalism began to distinguish themselves consciously from fundamentalism. These "new evangelicals" did share broad faith commitments with fundamentalists, notably an opposition to liberalism and a high seriousness in understanding the Bible and its relationship to a life of genuine discipleship. But unlike fundamentalists, they did not insist on separation and dispensationalism as measures of orthodoxy, nor were they rigidly intolerant of some doctrinal differences. This group, calling itself "evangelical" to distinguish itself from fundamentalism on the one hand and conciliar liberalism on the other, emerged formally in 1941 with the formation of the National Association of Evangelicals, which consciously sought to occupy a kind of middle theological ground.[13] Today new evangelicals are often urban, educated, theologically sophisticated, and socially conscious; are open to a moderately wide range of behavioral norms; and are reasonably willing to dialogue with persons whose faith stances they do not share. They value academic training. Gordon-Conwell in the East and Fuller Seminary in the West are their Harvard and Yale, with faculties that are producing a rich new body of sound theological scholarship. During the 1970s and 1980s, many of these evangelicals exhibited new openness to interdenominational dialogue, to science, and to biblical criticism; interest in wholistic spiritual nurture (as opposed merely to "saving souls"); and active, occasionally radical, involvement in issues of peace and justice.

Not all the heirs of nineteenth-century evangelicalism, however, followed the path toward either new evangelicalism or fundamentalism. A substantial number of "historic evangelicals"—many, though by no means all of them, from rural areas and from the lower and the lower middle classes—remained committed to a strong and simple faith that is firmly Christ-centered, personal, biblical, and occasionally anti-intellectual. Characterized by an affective, often revivalistic piety, these believers typically do not share the political and social concerns of their "evolved" brothers and sisters. Neither do they embrace rigid and doctrinally precise belief. Their theological concerns are implicit rather than formalized, and they seldom engage in disputation. Substantial numbers of them are diffused throughout most of the mainline churches, but many are also in independent fellowships and congregations. Historic evangelicals are well represented among predominantly black fellowships, where they are usually characterized by the title "Bible believing" rather than "evangelical."[14] In many ways these Christians are the real latter-day representatives of popular nineteenth-century evangelical Protestantism.

Pentecostals

Although the terms *pentecostal* and *charismatic* are often used to describe the same spirit-filled impulse, each is a historically and even theologically distinct movement. Classic American pentecostalism has its roots in late nineteenth- and early twentieth-century developments that emphasized sanctification, Christian holiness and perfection, dispensationalism, and faith healing. Like fundamentalists, and at roughly the same time, pentecostals responded to modern developments by looking backward, in this case to the spirit-filled, first-century church described in the Book of Acts.

The beginnings of American pentecostalism are usually traced to the Topeka, Kansas, revival that began at Charles F. Parham's Bethel Bible School in 1901, when eighteen-year-old Agnes Ozman began to speak in tongues. Parham concluded that tongue-speaking, or glossolalia, was evidence of being "baptized in the Holy Spirit,"[15] and his subsequent ministry took this pentecostal message across the South and Midwest. In 1906, William J. Seymour, a black Holiness minister influenced by Parham, began to preach the theory that the only true evidence of being baptized in the Spirit was speaking in tongues (Acts 2:4; 10:45–46; 19:6). This was a controversial teaching, because many Christians believed themselves to have been baptized in the Spirit at the time of conversion, or "entire sanctification." In a ramshackle warehouse on Azusa Street in Los Angeles, Seymour's revival began in April 1906, with tongue-speaking and healing as its central foci. From Azusa Street, the pentecostal impulse spread across America and eventually to Europe. In an era of harsh racial separation, both blacks and whites joined together in affirming the five central tenets of the movement: justification by faith, sanctification as a distinct work of grace, baptism in the Holy Spirit as evidenced by tongue-speaking, healing, and the "personal premillennial rapture of the saints at the second coming of Christ."[16]

This was at first an unusually harmonious and pluralistic movement involving blacks, whites, and Hispanics, as well as both male and female leadership. But controversies soon emerged over the Trinity, sanctification, and the significance of glossolalia. Some pentecostals established new denominations, of which the Assemblies of God and the predominantly black Church of God in Christ are perhaps best known. Others eschewed formal denominational affiliation, remaining local and independent. Today pentecostal churches attract members from a broad spectrum of racial, ethnic, educational, and social backgrounds. The worldwide movement is growing rapidly, particularly in the Third World, and its members are cautiously exploring contacts with mainline churches. In general, the pentecostal churches continue to emphasize the power of the Holy Spirit in individual lives, divine healing, and the purification of human nature from sin.

Charismatics

Now less than fifty years old, the charismatic movement is a relative newcomer within conservative Christianity. Contemporary charismatics are Christians who take at face value biblical accounts of the Holy Spirit's gifts, first proclaimed by Peter on the day of Pentecost and later detailed by Paul. Glossolalia is the most familiar of these charismata, but charismatics have the common understanding of spiritual gifts as including a variety of miraculous and nonmiraculous powers, such as faith, healing, wisdom, administration, prophecy, exhortation, and teaching. At its heart the charismatic experience is one of personal empowerment, a kind of holy disruption in a believer's life that transforms doubt into certainty, issuing in joyful and prayerful worship.

In emphasizing plural gifts, as well as in its unwillingness to identify tongue-speaking as an essential "second blessing," the charismatic movement differs markedly from classic pentecostalism. Its origins are different, also. Charismatics trace their beginnings to the late 1940s, when a few evangelists, including the young Oral Roberts, began to introduce spirit-baptized Christianity to audiences outside traditional pentecostal circles. During the next decade, primarily through Demos Shakarian's Full Gospel Business Men's Fellowship International, this ministry was enlarged; and a few people in different denominations experienced the baptism of the Holy Spirit. But it was the work of a California-based Episcopal priest, Dennis Bennett, that gave the movement its first national exposure. During the 1960s, the movement expanded rapidly into Protestant, Roman Catholic, and even Orthodox communities. Initially, most of the new charismatics chose to remain within their own fellowships as witnesses to and resources for the possibility of a revivified inward relationship with God. Their thrust was ecumenical. With Dennis Bennett they believed that "God is not interested in blessing any particular denomination or organization as such. The Church is one. . . . The Holy Spirit today is reaching into the structures that man has set up, ignoring our labels, and teaching and empowering those who are receptive."[17]

More recently the charismatic movement has produced a host of nondenominational, spirit-filled congregations and programs, including the well-known Melodyland Christian Center in Anaheim, California, and evangelist Pat Robertson's Christian Broadcasting Network. Particularly since the late 1970s, these nondenominational groups have multiplied rapidly, often affiliating with similar groups through associations or networks. Three evolutionary developments have also emerged since the 1980s. One is the new teaching of "signs and wonders" (the expectation of supernatural events and blessings) as a normal part of Christian life and evangelism. This teaching is especially popular among persons (now sometimes calling themselves the "third wave") whose spiritual gifts have not included glossolalia. A second is the growing fissure between renewal and restorationist charismatics (a distinction, incidentally, that is also present in contemporary pentecostalism). While the former—like the United Church of Christ's Focus Renewal Ministries—continue to work within their denominations of origin, the latter see these bodies as essentially unrenewable. Arguing for the reestablishment of the early church functions of apostles, prophets, and elders, restorationists often stress biblical inerrancy and strong, authoritative leadership.[18] Finally, a good number of nonrestorationist charismatics who have grown tired of fighting for acceptance and change in their denominations have exited to traditional pentecostal fellowships like the Assemblies of God, where they have contributed to growth and diversification.

Chapter 2

Religious Authority and the Churches

Why do some conservative Christians believe that the world was created in six twenty-four hour days? Why do many liberals believe that evolution is God's chosen way of effecting change? To answer these and other questions about the content of Christian belief, it is necessary to look at the sources of religious authority that undergird both conservative and liberal thought.

The word *authority* suggests the legitimate or recognized power of a person or agent to influence others. When we speak about religious authority, we are referring to those basic sources of power we acknowledge as influential in our Christian beliefs and behavior. All Christian beliefs are derived from some source of authority, and all Christians acknowledge sources of authority for their faith. But not all agree about the nature of that authority.

In part, this lack of agreement is a function of the complex nature of religious knowledge itself. For example, if Jesus were physically present today, it would seem logical to acknowledge his divine presence as the primary source of religious authority in our lives. But to do so would raise further questions. How would we determine that this man is authoritative for us and not some clever charlatan? Perhaps we would know because of our actual sensory experience of his charismatic presence. Or perhaps we would know through careful, reasoned assessment of his words and works. For the Jews of Jesus' own time, there were two additional ways of assessing Jesus' claims. One was by the Torah, the gathered writings that tell the story of the people of Israel and predict the coming of the Messiah. Another was through the habitual and common interpretation of those writings, passed down from generation to generation of rabbis, and familiar to the faithful.

Christian groups have typically recognized one or more of these different kinds of authority for their own faith: holy scriptures, both Old and New Testaments; tradition, that is, the accepted doctrines, creeds, and teachings of the church handed down over the centuries; human reason; and human experience. These four sources of authority have assumed particular importance because of the two-thousand-year hiatus between the life of the historical Jesus and the present-day church. In the physical absence of their founder, Christians require authoritative standards in order to maintain orthodox belief and behavior. But without a common understanding of authority, they have enjoyed little agreement about what these standards should be.

In the Roman Catholic church, believers have maintained authoritative standards primarily through the teaching office of the apostolic ministry. Roman Catholics believe that Jesus formally passed the mantle of his authority on to the apostles and through them to their official successors, the bishops and popes. Thus it is through the structure of the church itself that authenticity of belief has been adjudicated and authority wielded. Protestants, on the other hand—both conservative and liberal—have generally insisted that the authority of the apostles was unique and limited to the age of the early church. Since that time it has been the written words of scripture that have carried the authentic word by which Christians might be guided and judged. Through these "living words" the Christ and his true gospel are made present to believers by the work of the Holy Spirit upon human hearts and minds. Both Protestants and Catholics have recognized, to a greater or lesser degree, that human reason and experience also influence interpretation and understanding.

How, then, do these several sources of authority interact? Is any one of them truly normative, that is, is there a single source of authority that legitimates and judges the truth claims of the others? This is no simple issue, because in a practical sense, all four sources of authority function inevitably and inextricably together. For example, it is possible to argue from the theological perspective of *sola scriptura* that the Bible is the one authoritative source for

Christian faith. Nevertheless, interpretation of scripture involves both the experience a person has reading and interacting with the text itself and the accumulated experience brought to the reading. Moreover, the understanding and application of what is read is arguably dependent upon human powers of reason, as well as upon the particular biases and traditions of a reader influenced by time, place, and culture. Clearly the issue of religious authority is no simple matter, and it is perhaps the most basic source of controversy between conservative and liberal Christians. We shall examine each of the four sources of authority—scripture, experience, reason, tradition—in order to provide a foundation for our discussion of theology and doctrine in succeeding chapters.

Scripture

All Christians throughout the world acknowledge the Old and New Testaments as authoritative for their faith. But the scriptures do not have equal meaning and value for all. Indeed, to assert that the scriptures are authoritative for faith is to raise several very basic questions. Are all parts of the Bible authoritative, the Song of Solomon as well as the writings of Paul? Are all parts equally authoritative? What is the relationship between the Testaments? And what are we to make of those portions of the text that seem to contradict today's scientific and moral understandings, for example, the creation stories or the apparent acceptance of slavery? The many possible answers to these questions are a measure of the deep divisions within Christendom.

Some of these divisions are relatively recent. Although common use of the term *biblical inerrancy* is only about a century old, the concept itself is much older. For over two centuries Protestants accepted the absolute accuracy and veracity of the Bible as a given. When the English Puritans migrated to Massachusetts Bay, they came as fervent people of the Book, convinced that the Bible contained a thoroughgoing social blueprint for their experimental "city on a hill," as well as all the information necessary for faith and practice.

By the late 1700s, however, new scientific discoveries and new assumptions about human reason had begun to effect permanent changes in people's understanding of the Bible. Knowledge of the laws of nature cast doubt on the veracity of miracles; careful scholars found errors in biblical reporting and discrepancies in Old Testament prophecy. Some skeptics insisted that the Bible was merely a literary product not unlike other human works. In America, prominent architects of the new republic, including Benjamin Franklin and Thomas Jefferson, argued that human reason rendered divine revelation basically unnecessary. Nevertheless, it was not until after the Civil War that a combination of factors—Darwin's theories of evolution and natural selection, the so-called higher biblical criticism imported from Germany, and new geologic and archaeological discoveries—brought these radical, new ideas into prominence.

The result was religious crisis. Some Christians, to be sure, found the new thought perfectly compatible with their faith. The Bible, they argued, deals with broad and timeless truths about God, humankind, and faith; it is not an encyclopedic sourcebook for history and science. But others, like Princeton scholar Charles Hodge, were troubled and angered. "Grant one error in the Sacred Book and its authority is gone," declared Hodge.[1]

From the late 1880s on, Christians waged a full-scale "battle for the Bible" that has yet to be won. At issue was not only the nature of the scriptures but also the way they should properly be studied. Earlier (or lower) criticism had simply examined and compared scriptural texts carefully to determine their authenticity. But the new higher criticism insisted on an objective examination of historical sources, events, literary forms, and cultural presuppositions that presumably underlay the texts. Thus it questioned many cherished assumptions about the Bible, including, for instance, the Mosaic authorship of the Pentateuch and the authorship of several New Testament letters traditionally attributed to Paul.

Defenders of the higher criticism argued that Christian faith is not dependent upon an inerrant Bible, nor does a human hand in biblical authorship deny its divine inspiration; there is a difference between God's Word and the words that transmit it. The stream of scripture "brings down precious gold," wrote liberal Asa Gray, "but the water—the vehicle of transportation—is not gold."[2] The Bible, their opponents countered, speaks clearly about its own inspiration (see, for example, 2 Timothy 3:16), and this should be sufficient for any believer. Moreover, to admit that there are errors in scripture or that some parts are more worthy than others is to make each person his or her own authority; people then must judge the Bible, instead of the reverse.

During most of the twentieth century, these deep historic divisions have been virtually definitive of liberal and conservative positions. Among the latter group, however, there was notable consensus. Down to the early 1960s, most conservative Christians agreed that the Bible in its original manuscripts, or "autographs," was inerrant and fully God's word. Moreover, they insisted, the Bible was characterized by four definitive attributes. First, it is *inspired*. Although culture-bound human beings wrote the words of the texts, they were enabled to do so without error through the protective action of the Holy Spirit. Similarly, the Holy Spirit participated in the process of textual selection that led to the formalizing of the canon. Second, the scriptures may be described as having *plenary inspiration*. All parts of the Old and New Testaments are fully God's Word; all parts (despite the apparent obscurity and even distastefulness of some) have deliberately been included by God for our edification. Third, the texts are *verbally inspired*; that is, every single word is important to the whole. We are not simply to extract broad principles such as "God is love" from the text; rather we are to study each portion for what it actually says. The final attribute, the principle of *confluence*, governs our understanding of the nature of the texts. Just as in the person of Jesus the divine and human natures were fully and equally present, so the divine and human elements have interacted in the transmission of biblical texts. Thus the writers reliably reflect God's timeless intentions, but they also reveal their own unique personal and cultural perspectives.

Despite this early agreement over biblical inerrancy, con-servatives themselves have clashed over the way in which the inerrant scriptures ought to be interpreted. And as recently as 1972, the notion of inerrancy itself was challenged from within when Fuller Theological Seminary, in the rewriting of its state-ment of faith, signaled a major doctrinal shift. Fuller, located in Pasadena, California, had since its founding in 1947 been a bulwark of intelligent, self-proclaimed fundamentalism. But under the leadership of President David Hubbard it had moved gradually toward a more centrist evangelical position, advocating what eventually came to be called infallibilism or limited inerrancy.

The original Fuller statement expressed the predictable inerrantist position that the Bible was "free from all error in the whole or in the part." But the new statement of faith contained what to many conservatives were untenable modifications, asserting that "all the books of the Old and New Testaments, given by divine inspiration, are the written word of God, the only infallible rule of faith and practice."[3] By limiting the infallible authority of the Bible to matters relating directly to the believer and the church, this new scheme preserved biblical integrity even as it opened up the possibility of a more extensive and sophisticated use of critical methods.

Meanwhile, liberals, a majority of whom remained deeply convinced of the Bible's divine origins, had adopted a freer, more functional understanding of the Bible's authority and inspiration. That authority does not lie primarily in the Bible's facticity or in its nature as a sourcebook for ethics and morals. Rather, the Bible is authoritative because it transforms persons, bringing them into an encounter with the living God.

Today a whole spectrum of ways to understand the Bible exists. Of these, three are familiarly recognized, and a fourth seems to be emerging out of the encounter between new evangelicals and mainline Protestants.

As a group, *inerrantists* continue to represent the historic assertion that all parts of the Bible are wholly free from error. Yet within this most conservative category several variations may be discovered. Although few scholars hold to the so-called dictation theory of biblical authorship, at the popular level the notion that God literally dictated each word of the texts is not entirely uncommon. Far more common, however, are inerrantists (more familiarly called literalists) who read the scriptures with minimal scholarly or critical study. Literalists accept as factual the existence of real "first parents," Adam and Eve; the story of Jonah and the great fish; and the forecasts in the book of Revelation concerning the world's last days. Moreover, they argue that these accounts have been handed down reliably, through the intervention of the Holy Spirit, from the time of their original authorship (and through various translations) to the present. Often it is members of this group who champion the King James Version of the Bible or other conservatively sponsored translations; they believe renditions (such as the Revised Standard Version) produced by liberal scholars have not enjoyed the reliable protection of the Spirit.

More open-minded inerrantists stress the confluence of the human and divine natures in biblical authorship: the Holy Spirit has enabled individuals to record God's truth, but without disguising the distinctive character of their own personalities or cultures. Acknowledgment of both the human and the divine factors in the transmission of texts enables believers to maintain the integrity of an inerrantist position without insisting on literalism and without dismissing scholarly inquiry entirely. Because the texts have been mediated through human personalities and cultures, it is useful to be aware of the historical, literary, and theological factors that have influenced their transmission. Additionally, knowledge of the human factor permits an acceptable range of error, inexactness, and interpretation in biblical reporting. But because the texts are protected by the Holy Spirit, Christians can be certain that God's essential message has been preserved, despite the likelihood of reportorial errors. The most liberal inerrantists do not insist on a literal reading of texts but assume that often the Bible discloses inerrant *theological* statements rather than factual material. Thus in the seven-day account of creation, it is the description of God's involvement in bringing every part of the universe into being that is inerrant and not the specific number of days in which God is said to have worked and rested.

Infallibilists (or *limited inerrantists*) share with inerrantists a high view of the authority of scripture. But they do not assume that the texts are without error either in their original or in their transmitted forms. The new Fuller Seminary Statement of Faith, mentioned earlier, indicates this position clearly with its assertion that the scriptures are "the only infallible rule of faith and practice." The purpose of the Bible is to provide people with knowledge about ultimate things: the nature of God and humankind, the sacrifice of Christ, the way to salvation. We need not expect the Bible to be accurate or exact concerning science, history, or other areas of knowledge; in these matters, we may well expect the texts to reflect the primitive worldviews of their human writers.

As with inerrancy, the infallibilist position is not all of a piece. Its most conservative representatives argue that, despite the Bible's many interpretive voices and despite the many centuries over which it was transmitted, the Bible does speak with one single, sure, and reliable voice in matters essential for salvation. Other infallibilists admit that, even theologically, the Bible is not univocal, yet the heart of its saving message can be discerned by believers reading through the eye of faith. Some infallibilists develop this viewpoint more radically, arguing that this "essence" is to be discovered in the recorded actions and teachings of Jesus; these in turn serve as a touchstone for interpreting and asserting the rest of scripture.[4]

With the exception of all but the most rigid literalists, both inerrantists and infallibilists can be found throughout the various conservative denominations and fellowships, as well as in Protestant mainline and other Christian groups. A third position, however—sometimes designated *inspirationist* or *functionalist*—is most typical among liberal Protestants.

The inspirationist position, like the previous two, regards the scriptures with seriousness and asserts the primacy of the Bible's authority. But this position differs in important respects from the former ones. First, although inspirationists may speak of a central thematic core of scriptural teaching that is discernible by believers, they do not regard the essence of this core as comprising propositional truths. The inspirationist understanding of scripture is functional, not propositional: the Bible is authoritative, not because it offers truths *about* life, but because it directly *affects* life. Writes one interpreter: ". . . the truth of the Christian faith does not inhere in propositions. Its propositions are always invocations. The proper response to an invocation is not, 'I consent intellectually' or 'I believe it to be true.' It is a *sursum corda,* a lifting up of the heart in willing response."[5] Also, inspirationists are likely to emphasize the human rather than the supernatural dimension in both the transmission and the reception of scripture. Consequently, their assertion of the culturally relative nature of the texts is much more thoroughgoing. Inspirationists take for granted that even dogmatic and theological statements in the scriptures may be culture-bound and "in error" when measured against other sources of authority both without and within the Bible itself. Some contemporary inspirationists, particularly those influenced by feminist theology, regard the Bible with what is called a "hermeneutic of suspicion." While they recognize the existence of a deep core of essential truth, they believe it is so encrusted with the prejudices of centuries of male-dominated culture that the truth is extremely difficult to discern.

Unlike most inerrantists and infallibilists, inspirationists embrace a wide range of viewpoints concerning the supernatural nature of biblical accounts. Some inspirationists endorse a thoroughgoing supernaturalism, trusting in the full veracity of Jesus' miracles and the virgin birth. Others assume that these accounts represent explainable natural phenomena or the theologizing tendencies of the early church. In general, however, inspirationists are unlikely to claim that their faith or the authority of the Bible depends on supernatural understandings.

The fourth category of interpretation, which is a developing tendency more than a firmly established point of view, has been described by United Church of Christ evangelical Donald G. Bloesch and others.[6] *Catholic evangelicalism* is self-consciously inclusive of both evangelical and mainline concerns. In this understanding, scripture is the first and final source of authority for faith. But experience, reason, and tradition together are the instrumentalities by which scripture is engaged and understood. Unique in its combination of realism, openness, and seriousness with regard to the biblical texts, catholic evangelicalism holds out a real possibility of convergence between evangelical and mainline believers.

Experience

All Christians acknowledge, to a greater or lesser extent, their personal experience as a source or medium of religious authority. But the normative role of human experience remains a controversial and complex issue.

The term *experience* itself is elusive and can be understood at least three different ways. First, experience describes any immediate awareness of encounter with what may be identified as supernatural realities. Such encounters often provide the *focus* for analysis and reflection but they are not primarily *characterized* by analysis and reflection. The classic instance of this sort of experience is Paul's blinding conversion on the Damascus road, an experience that changed Paul's life and led him eventually to profound theological reflection. Similar experiences may include mystical encounters with God, tongue-speaking and other gifts of the Spirit, dreams and visions, life-after-life encounters, and even occult awareness of the "forces of darkness."

Second, experience may refer to any occurrence, activity, or situation in which an individual actually has participated. When William Wordsworth penned his famous line "The child is father of the man," he was referring to the cumulative and formative influence of life experience in shaping each human being. Every person's emotional, moral, and rational attitudes are undergirded and molded by a lifetime of accumulated, unique, and personal experience. These include hundreds of variables: education, family background, personal injuries and psychological traumas, pastoral role models, failure and success in business or romance, and many others. Experience in this sense refers not to the supernatural but to the eminently natural, day-to-date realities that shape human hearts and minds.

In a third context, experience can describe the whole cultural milieu in which a person or group operates. Here it is assumed that broadly systemic as well as intimately personal realities are significant in shaping human thought and belief. Race, gender, historical era, class or caste, nationality—these represent cultural variables that in subtle and often unconscious ways affect our religious ideas and practices.

Historically, and perhaps especially so in America, it is the first meaning of experience that is most familiar. From the Puritans to present-day charismatics, personal and private religious experience has been understood by many as an essential evidence, or seal, of one's faith. As noted previously, both the first and second Great Awakenings stressed the centrality of the religious affections in the life of faith, and today the revival tradition keeps alive similar convictions. Even an intellectual minority movement like nineteenth-century Transcendentalism represented, in part, a revolt against what Ralph Waldo Emerson referred to as the "corpse-cold," formal, and institutionalized Unitarianism of his day, in favor of a more immediate and personal faith.

However, during the twentieth century, growing awareness of the process of human development has focused attention on the nonprivatized dimension of experience. Theologians influenced by liberation thought emphasize that all meaningful theology must take as its starting point the cultural milieu of particular peoples. Indeed, they argue, the gospel is necessarily mediated through the interpretive lens of culture.

In all this the central issue is not whether experience is important, but whether it is assumed to be authoritative or normative, especially in relation to scripture. Does experience, understood in the widest sense, set the standard by which interpretive judgments are made, including judgments about the meaning of the Bible?

Among most conservatives the formal, negative response to this question is *sola scriptura;* that is, it is the Bible that serves as the first and final test of truth. Particularly among fundamentalist and evangelical groups with a strongly doctrinal and propositional bent, this insistence on the priority of scripture is stringent: the Christian's relationship to God is not based on experience but on obedience to timeless biblical truths. The danger in an exclusive appeal to experience is evident. It is self-deception and heresy. Conservatives correctly point out that it is the appeal to the experience of "personal revelation" that has historically produced heterodox and sectarian movements such as Mormonism, Christian Science, and contemporary "pseudo-Christian" movements such as the Unification Church.

At the informal or functional level, however, the answers are less clear. In practice, pentecostals, historic evangelicals, and some charismatics do elevate privatized experience to a kind of normative status. Pentecostals who insist on tongue-speaking as proof of saving faith; charismatics who look to the "leading of the Spirit" for all sorts of decision making; fundamentalists and evangelicals who insist on a definitive, born-again event—all these may use subjective experience as an unacknowledged but decisive standard for assessing and directing their faith.

Among mainline Protestants, experience is more readily acknowledged as authoritative. But most often this group uses the term *experience* to signify the totality of a person's cultural and personal context. Liberals tend to agree that, regardless of their spiritual state, all women and men are profoundly affected by a multitude of variables, which, whether they are aware of it or not, inevitably determine even the ways biblical truth is received and understood. In this very basic sense, experience really is ultimately authoritative, because no one can stand outside of its formative influence. Even the revelatory events described in the Bible are necessarily filtered through the lenses of particular human experience.

In theory liberals do not assert the primacy of experiential over scriptural authority. Theirs may best be described as a wholistic viewpoint in which meaning, authority, and truth inhere neither in the isolated words of scripture nor in privatized experience, but in the whole life of the experiencing, interpreting, worshiping community of faith. Nevertheless, liberals too risk unconsciously elevating the authority of experience when their concern for context subsumes their attention to scriptural content.

Reason

When the early Christian leader Tertullian asked the famous question "What has Athens to do with Jerusalem?" he was commenting on the complex relationship between reason and revelation, between the "head" and the "heart." Despite the biblical admonition to "love the Lord your God with all of your heart, and all of your soul, and all of your mind," Christians have often found it difficult to discover the appropriate balance between these very different ways of knowing and understanding.

As a category of religious authority, reason has two distinct but closely related dimensions. Most simply, *reason* suggests careful, rational analysis. Serious scholarship that attempts to explore important theological issues (such as the meaning of the Trinity or the nature of Christ's sacrifice) represents the use of reason as a tool for the life of the church. When Christians use reason in this sense, they implicitly indicate their belief that it is appropriate to examine all of life, its religious as well as its secular mysteries, by means of rigorous inquiry. But reason need not be understood as the prerogative of scholars only. Whenever Christians think theologically—that is, when they attempt to understand and reflect critically, rather than merely accept unquestioningly—they are using reason as a tool of faith.

To claim that reason is a tool of faith, however, begs important questions. How reliable is the human mind when it seeks after the things of God? And what is the relationship of reason and reflection to revelation? In America, the answers to these questions have often signaled the line of demarcation between liberal and conservative thinkers. It has not always been so, however. The New England Puritans firmly insisted on the necessary connection between the head and the heart. In early New England, learning and experience were partners in the life of faith. Harvard and Yale were the products of the Puritans' fervent desire to perpetuate a learned as well as a pious ministry. Yet it was not long before the tension between head and heart, so delicately balanced, broke down.

During the 1740s, the Great Awakening, with its renewed emphasis on conversion and the religious affections, promoted vigorous anti-intellectual sentiments among many Christians. It was not far from the New Light assertion that God's grace is accessible to even the simplest and most uneducated person, to an understanding that knowledge and learning are irrelevant for a life of true faith. Ironically, at roughly the same time, liberal intellectual currents from Europe had the effect of elevating human reason over revelation as the supreme source of religious authority. Some few prominent thinkers (called Deists by their colleagues and "infidels" by their critics) now asserted that through the powers of reason alone human beings could ascertain the essentials of religious truth, including the existence of an omniscient, benevolent deity; the rules for appropriate human conduct; and even the reality of an afterlife with a system of rewards and punishments. Supernatural revelation was simply unnecessary. Finally, as noted earlier, a growing awareness during the nineteenth century that knowledge in the form of scientific inquiry led some Christians away from long-treasured biblical teachings convinced many that reliance on the discoveries of reason was tantamount to atheism. Consequently, as historian Richard Hofstadter has pointed out, "the churches withdrew from intellectual encounters with the secular world, gave up the idea that religion is a part of the whole life of intellectual experience, and often abandoned the field of rational studies on the assumption that they were the natural province of science alone."[7]

While twentieth-century modernists continued to embrace this "dangerous" sort of inquiry, adapting their theologies to the contemporary milieu, conservatives in general opted to devote their intellectual energies to evangelistic and polemical works. With the evangelical resurgence of the 1970s and 1980s, and as conservatives develop newly self-critical postures, this has begun to change. Systematic theologian John Jefferson Davis of Gordon-Conwell Theological School argues that "American evangelicals in this century have not adequately appreciated the importance of rational analysis and intellectual rigor for effectively penetrating the culture for Christ. . . . The evangelical tradition, focusing largely on personal religious experience, has not been effective in challenging the reigning ideologies entrenched in the institutions that command the heights of American culture."[8]

Although conservative Christians have begun to undertake serious theological work with new vigor, it is clear that for most of these thinkers, reason is not a locus of authority but a servant of the authoritative word discernible in the scriptures. Moreover, a substantial number believe that the efficacy of reason in exploring and understanding scripture is directly related to the spiritual state of the person exploring. John Jefferson Davis speaks for many: "Spiritual truth is understood only by those who have received the Spirit of God (1 Corinthians 2:14)."[9] To the unregenerate reason (that is the mind of an unconverted man or woman) gospel truths are merely "folly and stumbling blocks." Therefore, reason may be an important but conditionally reliable tool even for those conservative Christians who have embraced critical theological inquiry.

For modern liberals as well as for conservatives, reason tends to play a supporting role, auxiliary to scripture and experience. Some theologians, like Paul Tillich and Charles Hartshorne, have understood that unaided reason provides basic information about God and life. But few liberals today believe that reason alone is an adequate or sufficient source of religious understanding.

Nevertheless, the importance of reason should not be discounted. Like their Enlightenment forebears who distinguished among ideas that are according to reason, contradictory to reason, and above reason but not contradictory to it, liberals do use reason as an informal measure of the truth of religious claims. Reason may be invoked, for example, to argue against certain claims of faith healing or "special providences." More important, reason continues to be understood as an essential, God-given tool for inquiry. Typically mainline Protestants do not distinguish between regenerate and unregenerate reason. In part this is because many view the Christian life as a process of becoming rather than as a status or goal to be achieved. Thus reason can be understood as intrinsically good but also limited and subject to sin. "Now we understand in part": regardless of their spiritual state, human beings will always be flawed and finite in their rational powers. Even the most spiritual man or woman is never assured of knowing truth in its entirety. Error is endemic to humankind. Nevertheless, because even partial knowledge is a good gift of God's creation, reason may be used appropriately and reliably (and with proper humility) in our inquiries about both sacred and secular matters.

Tradition

At least three distinct understandings of *tradition* can be identified. In its oldest and most familiar usage, tradition (usually spelled with a capital "T") refers to the corpus of doctrines, teachings, customs, worship practices, and interpretations of scripture that have been transmitted by the whole body of Christ from its earliest days to the present. The Apostles' and Nicene Creeds are representative of this Tradition in that they continue to serve as standards by which orthodoxy may be assessed.

A second usage refers to any of the particular groups or denominations that came into being before and after the Reformation, together with the practices and beliefs that formally distinguish or define them. Thus believer's baptism and immersion are practiced in the Baptist "tradition." A final meaning designates the accumulated customs, teachings, and practices that characterize different denominational groups and that often wield significant informal authority within them. Basic to this meaning of tradition is the understanding that churches are always involved in the "traditioning" process, establishing customs and teachings that have authoritative force within their particular communions. For example, in the United Church of Christ, a twentieth-century merger of four distinct historical groups, an early commitment to becoming a "united and uniting" fellowship has influenced ongoing ecumenical activities and conversations with other denominations. Thus this commitment has become a tradition with normative force for the denomination. [10]

In their 1980 study of American religion, researchers George Gallup, Jr., and David Poling reported a significant difference between Roman Catholics and Protestants on the issue of tradition. While 70 percent of Catholic priests accepted "what the church says" as ultimately authoritative, an equal number of Protestant clergy (76 percent) opted for "what the Bible says" as their final authority. [11] For both liberal and conservative Protestants, the formal authority of tradition, when it has been recognized at all, has clearly been subordinated to that of the scriptures. [12]

In America, what has sometimes been described as a characteristically ahistorical mentality has contributed to this general Protestant mistrust of tradition. Revivalism, with its insistence on conversion and personal decision, has reinforced the tendency. Why should people pay attention to ancient teachings, creeds, or doctrines when all that is necessary for life and salvation is a decision for Christ? Moreover, the restorationist, or "repristinationist," leanings of some Protestant groups (that is, their desire to return to the presumably pure practices and beliefs of the first-century church) has sometimes led to the effective dismissal of centuries of church history. [13]

In all this, conservatives and mainline Protestants share fundamental attitudes toward tradition, more so than with respect to any of the other areas of authority. Still, there are differences. Some mainline denominations—including, for example, Lutherans, Presbyterians, and Episcopalians—are explicitly confessional in nature. These bodies do typically look to specific ancient formulas as authoritative. Mainline believers in general, because of their greater emphasis on the corporate nature of the church, are much more likely to accept the church's legitimate role in distinguishing false from authentic belief or interpretation. Common use of creeds and confessions in many of these denominations represents at least a tacit acknowledgment of the normative force of tradition. Conservatives, who insist on the doctrine of *sola scriptura,* find such an acknowledgment far less acceptable, although with the rise of self-consciously confessional evangelicalism this attitude most likely will change.

Chapter 3

The Individual Believer

Exactly what is the good news that the gospel proclaims? Although this question is a basic one for every Christian, it can be answered in many different ways. For some, the gospel is a profoundly social message, the news of God's incipient realm on earth. For others, it is the message of divine forgiveness that calls women and men to repentance and reconciliation. For still others, it is news of liberation, of freedom from bondage and oppression. To conservative Christians, it is perhaps above all the message of personal salvation that is found in the familiar and beloved words of John 3:16: "For God so loved the world that he gave his only Son, that whoever believes in him should not perish but have eternal life."

At the heart of a conservative reading of the gospel is the understanding that God's primary concern for humankind is not with its societies or systems or ecclesiastical structures, but with individual believers. This does not mean, necessarily, that conservatives are unconcerned with social issues or the wider church. As scholars like Nazarene Timothy Smith have pointed out, there is a rich historical tradition in America linking evangelical piety and social reform.[1] Yet for the majority of conservatives, it is the individual Christian who is the primary datum in any consideration of the meaning of faith. God first changes individual hearts, and it is through these "new" persons that the church may be built up and meaningful change effected.

A person "becomes new" through conversion. The scriptures say clearly that "unless one is born anew, one cannot see the kingdom of God [John 3:3]." Thus conservative believers insist on conversion as the *sine qua non* of legitimate, saving faith. This insistence is no twentieth-century innovation. For the New England Puritans, not only church membership but suffrage and other civil privileges were predicated on a person's having, and publicly describing, just such a change of heart. In the tradition of nineteenth-century revivalism, a similar change, though less surprising, more manipulable and predictable, was the goal of impassioned preaching.

Despite its historical importance, however, conversion has for the most part resisted rigid delimitation, for people's actual experiences have varied widely. Jonathan Edwards, the great eighteenth-century American theologian, described not one but several experiences that offered him hope of salvation. Even the seventeenth-century Puritans recognized the range of human possibility in their descriptions of a variable process of "preparation for salvation."

Today most conservatives do not insist on a rigid model for true conversion. But almost universally they expect that a person will have an identifiable moment of decision, a point at which he or she consciously makes a commitment to Jesus as personal Lord and Savior. This expectation represents a significant departure from the practice of mainline Protestants, who generally accept the nineteenth-century assumption that, with proper Christian nurture, it is possible for a person to "never not be a Christian."[2] Family devotions and guidance, Sunday School teaching, Bible study, sacramental observances—in the historic Protestant churches these provide the nurturing context in which a young woman or man may mature in the faith, never living outside it. To be sure, millions of mainline Christians have themselves had conversion and other powerful faith experiences. But few insist that such experiences, which serve to strengthen and broaden faith commitments, are in any way definitive of being Christian.

An emphasis on conversion as the point of entry into faith leads naturally to several concerns. The title of Billy Graham's popular book *How to Be Born Again* (1977) reveals one of them: if conversion, or being "born again," is essential to being Christian, then how can a would-be Christian make it happen? For Protestants, this is a delicate issue. Since the Reformation, orthodox Protestantism has affirmed the doctrine of justification by faith alone, by which is meant that salvation can never be bought through any good works or merit of our own. Rather, God in mercy justifies us (deals with us as if we were ourselves just and righteous people) even though in truth no one can keep from sinful thoughts and acts. Thus the redemptive activity in salvation belongs wholly to God. Nevertheless, evangelicals, particularly those who are heirs of the revival tradition, have long assumed that the process of salvation involves at least some human act of will. This does not represent a compromise of the principles of *sola gratia, sola fide* (grace alone, faith alone); rather it is a recognition that human responsiveness is a critical factor in the process. God freely offers the Son to undeserving sinners. But they must first be aware of the nature of the gift being offered, and they can receive the Son only by a personal decision to do so. An analogous image is that of feeding hungry persons. Bread can be placed in their hands, but unless they know what it is and are willing to chew and swallow it, they will receive no nourishment.

Because of this crucial interaction between divine initiative and human response, it becomes essential to prepare people for God's gracious offer of salvation. Consequently, conservative Christians have developed a variety of popular, standardized guidelines to facilitate the process. There is no "tidy little formula" for receiving salvation, warns Billy Graham. But Bill Bright, founder of the well-known Campus Crusade for Christ, is less cautious. In his widely distributed tract *The Four Spiritual Laws,* Bright writes that "just as there are physical laws that govern the physical universe, so there are spiritual laws which govern your relationship with God." By following the "four laws" and acknowledging their truth, a person may receive Christ.[3]

Because not every decision for Christ is accompanied by a crisis experience or by continuous heightened emotions, it is often impossible for a new Christian actually to feel the stirrings of altered selfhood within. A second concern for conservatives, then, is with the issue of what actually happens when a person turns to Christ and is changed. How can a person be sure he or she is truly saved?

The biblical word for conversion, *metanoia,* suggests more than a single, momentary event. Instead it indicates something like an ongoing process whose first fruits are evidenced in a transformed life-style. This process, by which the changed heart manifests itself in changed behavior, is usually called sanctification. For the New England Puritans, "sanctification is evidence of justification" was axiomatic. To help determine the state of a person's soul, at least insofar as this is humanly possible, one scrutinized his or her conduct. Similarly, many contemporary conservatives assume that a proper Christian life-style, however this may be defined, is both a result of and a logical illustration of the justification and regeneration experienced initially in conversion. Conduct, in other words, is a trustworthy external sign by which a person's spiritual state and growth can be measured.

But this is an area in which notably and often intricately different theological understandings exist among conservatives. At least four distinct points of view can be identified concerning the changes that take place in a believer's life.[4] There are conservatives who believe that sanctification takes place after and because of the new birth experienced in conversion. A woman or man grows in grace, slowly becoming purer in thought and more Christ-like in deed. (Precisely what the nature of the relationship is between justification and sanctification, however, may not be spelled out). Other conservatives have been strongly influenced by the nineteenth-century Holiness Movement, which was in part an outgrowth of Methodist founder John Wesley's teachings about the possibility of Christian perfection, or sinlessness, in this life. These evangelicals view perfection as a discrete, instantaneous event that is distinct from and subsequent to the regeneration of the heart that takes place initially in conversion. Although they too may emphasize growth in grace, it is the so-called second blessing of perfection to which they look as an evidential event.

A third group, also influenced by the Holiness Movement, followed the distinctive teachings of Dwight W. Moody and other evangelists associated with the famous Keswick holiness conferences in England during the latter part of the nineteenth century. These evangelists discounted the possibility of the total elimination of sin but emphasized the Holy Spirit's empowerment for "victory" in personal life. Combined with a strong premillennial worldview, these teachings focused on the personal and individual dimensions of Christian life and excluded its broader social and ethical implications. In this early alliance between premillennialism and holiness thought, it is possible to discern themes that inform contemporary fundamentalism.[5]

This diversity is complicated further by the fact that a fourth perspective, that of pentecostalism, is itself divided by several different viewpoints. In the earliest tradition of classic pentecostalism, conversion was thought to be an elongated process, involving three different "works," or steps. The first work, justification, offered regeneration and the remission of sins, while a second work, sanctification, imparted holiness. A third work, the Baptism of the Holy Spirit (evidenced by tongue-speaking), represented a "gift of power," an additional work of grace that enabled and empowered the spiritual life. Later pentecostal teachings deemphasized sanctification as a distinct work, while continuing to view the Baptism of the Holy Spirit as separate from conversion and subsequent to it. Some contemporary pentecostals, however, argue that it is preferable to speak of the Baptism of the Holy Spirit not as a distinct work but as an event that actualizes the fullness of grace already given to a believer.

To mainline Christians, the precision and care with which these distinctions are outlined (and indeed, their historically divisive nature) may seem utterly baffling. Yet it is precisely the diligence with which conservatives have charted the conversion process that reveals their deep longing for the assurance that faith and its fruits are not illusory but real.

In this quest for assurance we may discern a final, crucial question for conservative believers: How is the Christian life to be understood and lived in such a way that it provides a modicum of certainty? Recent study suggests that the traditional world-denying life-style of conservative Christianity has been modified somewhat as secular and liberal values have impacted new generations of believers.[6] Even so, it is the insistence on a proper Christian life, on right conduct (or, as it is sometimes called, orthopraxy), that distinguishes faithful conservatives. Several historic factors underlie this concern: the characteristic dualism of conservative thought; the influence of holiness teachings, with their emphasis on actualized perfection; the heritage and continuing influence of American Puritanism, with its work ethic and emphasis on godly conduct. But to understand the theological assumptions that lie behind the focus on right conduct, it is necessary to look again at the conversion process.

In his thoroughgoing study, *The Evangelical Movement: Growth, Impact, Controversy, Dialogue,* Mark Ellingsen suggests that historically there have been two ways of understanding what actually happens when believers are justified. According to one model, which Ellingsen calls "union with conformity to Christ" and which is most typical in the mainline Protestant churches, baptized believers are united with Christ through their baptisms and so receive all Christ's gifts: grace, life, salvation. Thereafter, their lives reflect a natural and spontaneous—though of course imperfect—expression of conformity to Christ. The details of the Christian life thus "do not require explicit attention any more than happily married couples require rigid rules to nurture their loving relationship"; in fact, rigid standards and rules may interfere with their real growth and maturity.

A second understanding of justification employs what Ellingsen refers to as a "forensic" or juridical metaphor. In this model, more typical among conservatives, God as judge pronounces a verdict of "not guilty," although the defendants really have committed the crimes of sin and selfishness of which they are accused. Thus in a kind of legal fiction the defendants are simply regarded as innocent. In some instances justification and sanctification may be perceived as logically separate, while in others the conceptual relationship between the two is simply unclear. In either case, however, the conclusion is the same: if the Christian life is not directly affected by justification, then it must be fostered and supported by formal descriptions, guidelines, and rules.[7]

Not surprisingly, then, conservatives tend to delineate much more thoroughly than do mainline Protestants the specific kinds of behavior and attitudes that befit a Christian man or woman. This practice is undergirded by an appeal to biblical texts such as Matthew 5, which encourage the strict regulation of behavior and indicate the consequences of both obedience and disobedience: "Whoever then relaxes one of the least of these commandments and teaches so, shall be called least in the kingdom of heaven; but the one who does them and teaches them shall be called great in the kingdom of heaven."

Nevertheless, conservative attitudes toward the Christian life are not all of a piece. Among fundamentalists and some historic evangelicals and pentecostals, the biblical injunction to "come out from them, and be separate from them [2 Cor. 6:17]" is taken literally. Thus emphasis is placed on proscribing sinful behaviors that must be shunned in order for a person to remain faithful. A Christian is expected to renounce not only the predictable illicit pleasures and sins of the flesh (drinking, fornication, adultery, drugs, smoking, and even dancing and "Hollywood movies") but also those behaviors that undermine usefulness and productivity, such as idleness and profligacy. Strict moral fidelity in these proscribed areas is both a mark of salvation and a means by which the boundaries of worshiping congregations and communities may be strictly maintained.[8]

Among moderate conservatives, the emphasis may be on what *is* appropriate to the Christian life rather than what is not. Prescriptive guidelines, often highly systematized, typically suggest that Christians are distinguished by participation in the three essential activities of Bible study, prayer, and witnessing, as well as by attributes such as personal confidence and joy.

Basic for virtually all conservatives is the expectation that regular, prayerful reading of the Bible is a cornerstone of faith. Read by some as a blueprint for behavior, by others for an open-ended encounter with God, the Bible is accessible to everyone. Not everyone, however, will understand its deep truths or seek them diligently, for these are discernible only through the eyes of faith. Bible study, of course, is a universal part of church programming in mainline as well as conservative churches. But a growing literature of conservative self-help guidelines for independent scriptural study includes, for example, suggestions for enhancing the experience through preliminary prayer, regularity of time and place, memorization of texts, and meditation on God's message and its personal meaning. On the whole, conservative churches enjoy a membership that is far more biblically literate than that of the Protestant mainline.

Like Bible study, prayer is a daily activity that is to be undertaken in a disciplined and regular fashion. Prayer may be described in a variety of ways: as intercession, petition, listening, emptying or silence, discernment, confession, praise, or simply conversation with God. For most conservatives prayer is also spontaneous. Formal prayer, even in worship settings, is often dismissed as cold and impersonal. Somewhat ironically, this spontaneity may find expression via standard mnemonic formulas, such as Bill Bright's ACTS (adoration, confession, thanksgiving, supplication) or PRAY (praise, remember, ask, yield).

A third characteristic of the Christian life is witnessing. Public testimony of one's faith has long been a Christian tradition and remains so. Today, however, witnessing may also involve careful and sophisticated planning for results. Evangelism strategists like D. James Kennedy routinely employ the language of product and market to describe effective techniques for confronting and winning converts.[9] Contemporary evangelicals, especially those who have been nurtured in youth and campus organizations, may even see themselves as "salespersons for Christ," whose successes or failures verify their own spiritual status.

Not all the components of Christian living are as clearly delineated, or as universal, as these three activities. A newer thrust, encouraged by the ministries of Robert Schuller and others, offers a kind of christianized version of "human potential" thought. In this perspective, a decision for Christ should naturally effect positive changes in one's sense of self and self-worth and consequently in one's ability to serve. In his widely distributed book, *Self-Esteem: The New Reformation* (which was sent free to religious leaders and educators across America), Schuller writes: "The core of sin is a lack of self-esteem . . . to be saved is to know that Christ forgives me and now I dare to believe that I am somebody and I can do something for God and my fellow human beings."[10] Although Schuller's understanding of sin and salvation is, to say the least, unorthodox, his views are popular, perhaps especially among persons who find in them a legitimate Christian reading of current secular pop psychology.

But the above is by no means an exhaustive description of the Christian life within the broad conservative fellowship. There are a host of other possible expectations. For left-wing evangelicals, real faithfulness involves heightened concern and action on behalf of the oppressed, the poor, and the hungry. For evangelicals associated with the historical peace churches (Mennonites, Brethren, Friends), it demands visible commitment to peace, justice, and simplified living. For charismatics and pentecostals, it is evidenced by a pervasive spirituality that manifests itself in quiet personal joy and exuberant public worship. In its more extreme forms, it can include the expectation that the lives of the faithful will be blessed and rewarded with personal success, material prosperity, and physical health.

In their intense focus on the Christian life, conservative Christians are distinctly different from liberals. This difference is heightened by several factors within the latter group: the rationalist predisposition to downplay "supernatural" thinking; the heritage of the nineteenth-century Social Gospel, which emphasized the relation between salvation and social evil, rather than personal morality; the general rejection of dualism and prescriptive categories for behavior. But there are also two important theological differences. First, in the mainline churches it is not only the individual Christian but the whole fellowship of believers, the church, that is central theologically. We will discuss this more fully in chapter 4. But it is evident that by shifting focus from the individual believer and his or her salvation to the whole body of Christ, mainline Protestants de-emphasize the issue of personal piety and morality.

Second, the mainline denominations, as well as Roman Catholic and Orthodox communities, represent what is generally called the sacramental tradition. In sacramental theology, a believer does not enter the faith and fellowship through conversion. Instead persons receive the gifts of the Spirit through water baptism, whether of infants or adults, by sprinkling or immersion.

There is, of course, a long history of controversy over baptism within the sacramental churches themselves. Nevertheless, the groundbreaking 1982 document *Baptism, Eucharist, and Ministry (BEM),* prepared by the Faith and Order Commission of the World Council of Churches, reveals a genuine convergence among these groups. BEM describes baptism as a rite that "unites the one baptized with Christ and with his people" and that represents a washing away of sin, a new birth, a renewal by the Spirit, and a "liberation into a new humanity in which barriers of division whether of sex or race or social status are transcended." Baptized Christians are "pardoned, cleansed and sanctified by Christ, and are given as part of their baptismal experience a new ethical orientation under the guidance of the Holy Spirit."[11] In other words, in the sacramental action of baptism are contained all the elements of *metanoia,* or conversion, including regeneration, baptism by the Holy Spirit, and sanctification. It is true that differences remain over the issue of where, exactly, the "sign of the gift of the Spirit" may be found. For some it is in the sprinkling or immersion itself, for others (in the case of infant baptism) it is in rites of confirmation, and for still others it is in the process that encompasses both. But what is clear is that baptism, understood thus broadly, offers believers assurance of salvation that is full and final.

But how, specifically, do mainline Protestants understand this assurance? First, the gifts offered in baptism are said to be given *ex opere operato,* that is, baptism "works by working"; its efficacy is not dependent upon any external factors that relate to either the subject or the celebrant of the rite. Thus a child baptized in infancy, nurtured in a Christian environment in youth, and confirmed in adulthood need not hope for a crisis to confirm and seal his or her faith. [12] Second, the expectation that each baptized member of the body of Christ will at appropriate times choose regularly to receive the Lord's Supper as "assurance of the forgiveness of sins and the pledge of eternal life"[13] means that Christians in these traditions may feel continuously reassured about, and renewed in, their relationship with God. Third, since all God's gifts are bestowed with baptism, the baptized Christian need not design elaborate guidelines and structures for the assurance of salvation or the direction of a proper Christian lifestyle. It is enough that faith be present. Finally, for all these reasons, mainline Christians are rarely preoccupied with the distinction between nominal and real Christians, between those who merely claim to be of God, and those who really are. Because through faith and the sacraments full Christian reality is conveyed, there are no nominal Christians. Without this distinction, the need to maintain carefully constructed boundaries between saved and unsaved is diminished, as is the need to manifest personally the marks of one's legitimacy as a believer.

Chapter 4

The Church and Its Work

Since the time of the Protestant Reformation, one of the most basic questions for Christians has been one of the most difficult and divisive to answer: What is the church? The existence of hundreds of different denominations and fellowships reveals the complexity of this issue. Nor is it difficult to see why it is complex. What the church is understood to be is largely determinative of what the church does and says. For example, if those of a particular tradition understand their tradition essentially as a gathered community of born-again believers, they will engage in different activities and emphasize different theological issues from those of a tradition that understand themselves as holy bearers of the apostolic faith. The theologies, worship practices, mission goals, and evangelistic, or justice, activities that characterize (and divide) Christian groups are directly related to their ecclesiologies, or doctrines of the church.

Because Christians understand themselves in various ways as *church,* they share different and conflicting assumptions about church life and work. And, even more significant, because many Christians are unaware of their basic ecclesiological differences (indeed, are unaware that there *are* various ways to define *church*), it is often impossible for them to converse meaningfully together. Our ecclesial "languages" are widely disparate, beginning from varied starting points and appealing to different authorities for validation.

Lesslie Newbigin and Peter Schmiechen have identified five models of the church that are typically represented in American denominational life. As with all models, these are not pure types, but they may be found mixed within the same denominations or communions. The five models may be characterized by the following summary descriptions.

Participation in the historic community. This model stresses continuity of faith with the apostolic church and lodges authority in the offices and structures of the church itself.

Confessing the true faith. The mandate of the church is to proclaim and live by the gospel; its authority is scripture and/or creeds, which maintain gospel purity.

Rebirth in the Spirit. The church is a fellowship of persons born again and empowered by the Holy Spirit; its authority lies in the visible demonstration of these experiences.

Acts of justice and love. The church is a community engaged in "right action," whose love and service reach out to the oppressed and needy; its authority flows from the biblical mandate to serve.

Participation in an ecumenical vision. The church hears and responds to the call of oneness in Christ, believing that unity fosters renewal of all humankind; its authority is the scriptural and historical vision of unity. [1]

It will be evident from the discussion in previous chapters that conservative Christians tend to fit into the models of confession and rebirth, while mainline Christians more often affirm those of the historic community, activism, and ecumenism. Conservatives have generally understood the church as a fellowship or assembly of individual believers, with emphasis on the believers themselves. In this view, the church, though founded by Christ, is essentially a human institution that has reality and existence by virtue of its members, who are confessionally and spiritually "pure." In the case of some extreme independent congregations, the church may be perceived as little more than a local association that facilitates the prayer and worship life of individual Christians. Connectionalism and denominationalism are shunned because, in the words of Jerry Falwell, "We are at our best when we are free from hierarchical structures that would tie us down to denominational mediocrity. We are our own people."[2] Evangelical Carl F. H. Henry is theologically more explicit, asserting that if the Bible were to survive, but the church disappear, God's saving work would continue without it. [3]

By contrast, most mainline Christians believe that the church has its own objective reality. It was founded by Christ, and it thus has independent existence. It is not separate from God's saving work but is actually an instrumental part of it. Moreover, the church in its local manifestations is characterized by certain marks, or signs, that indicate it is the true church. Depending on the particular tradition, these marks may include the pure teaching of the gospel, the proper administration of the sacraments, the administration of discipline, and (most recently) racial and social inclusivity. The church is "one, holy, catholic, and apostolic"; it is united in time and across barriers of nationality and even belief because of its reality as a holy gift of God. To be sure, there are important differences among Reformed, Lutheran, and Roman Catholic traditions with respect to the nature of the church. But in general, believers in these traditions regard the church as a divine creation of God, rather than as a human fellowship that is entirely dependent upon a righteous constituency.

The conservative focus on the church as a community of regenerate believers is clearly related to several historical patterns of belief discussed previously. The Reformation heritage of protest against the monolithic and authoritative Roman Catholic system predisposed many to redefine the church in terms of regenerate membership. Revivalism, with its insistence on a decision for Christ, has long de-emphasized the corporate and salvific nature of the church in favor of an individualistic, personal gospel of salvation. Similarly, the doctrine of *sola scriptura*, often rigidly held, has discouraged any serious inclination to understand the church as a real and independent instrumentality through which God's gifts may be given and received. For all these reasons, conservatives for the most part have paid very little attention to the development of a broad and coherent doctrine of the church.

There are indications that this disregard is changing, however. Evangelical Donald G. Bloesch, lamenting "the appalling neglect of ecclesiology in the circles of conservative evangelicalism," writes that it is important for evangelicals to remember "that the church is not many but one, that it is not parochial but universal, that it has apostolic foundation and therefore antedates the Reformation and the great revivals."[4] The recent advent of evangelical and pentecostal dialogues with both the Roman Catholic and Protestant mainline bodies suggests a new openness among some conservatives to recognize alternative understandings of the church. Charismatics, many of whom have remained in mainline churches, often share liberal enthusiasm for ecumenical opportunities, particularly as they relate to evangelism. Fundamentalists, however, continue to be resolutely individualistic and separatistic. Indeed, the issue of ecclesial separation is one that marks a major boundary line between fundamentalists and other conservative believers. With premillennial dispensationalism, it is one of the marks of contemporary orthodox fundamentalism.

Separatism

Despite the adamancy with which it is held today, the "formal" doctrine of separation is of relatively recent origin, dating back roughly to the time of the fundamentalist-evangelical split. Several watershed events during the 1940s and 1950s precipitated the hardening into dogma of the separatist impulse. In 1941 and 1942 the rival Council of Christian Churches in America and the National Association of Evangelicals were organized, with separation a major source of contention between them. Six years later Harold John Ockenga, one of the founders of the NAE and pastor of Boston's venerable Park Street Congregational Church, delivered the convocation address at the opening of Fuller Theological Seminary in California. Calling for a new, responsible, and involved evangelicalism that would literally transform Western culture, Ockenga explicitly rejected the negativism and "come-outism" of his separatist colleagues. In their place, he outlined a new, engaging agenda that involved encounter rather than avoidance. Its purpose was "to recapture the denominational leadership from the inside by infiltration instead of frontal attack, to achieve respectability for othodoxy, and to attain societal reforms."[5]

For many fundamentalists, this was clearly heresy. What Ockenga advocated was nothing less than tolerance, which, in the definitive words of one critic, "leads to cooperation with error, contamination by error, and ultimate capitulation to error."[6]

The battle lines, however, had been drawn; and in 1957 the split was solidified around the issue of "ecumenical" or "cooperative" evangelism. In that year Billy Graham, a self-professed militant fundamentalist since early in his career, voluntarily cooperated with liberal church leaders in the sponsorship of his New York City crusade. Subsequently, he revealed a continuing leftward drift, associating in ministry events with liberals and Roman Catholics, and even attending a conference sponsored by the World Council of Churches.

What was the nature of this issue over which fundamentalists and evangelicals clashed, and which still engenders debate within the ranks of fundamentalism itself? *Separation* and *separatism* refer to the belief that God calls Christians to dissociate from persons who are not truly of the faith, perhaps especially from those who claim to be of the faith but are not fundamentalist otherwise in their doctrine and behavior. Numerous biblical passages underwrite a separatistic stance. For example, 2 Corinthians 6:17 admonishes: "Therefore come out from them, and be separate from them, says the Lord, and touch nothing unclean; then I will welcome you." Another key passage for fundamentalists is Romans 16:17, which adjures the faithful "to take note of those who create dissension and difficulties, in opposition to the doctrine which you have been taught; avoid them."

From the latter verse, fundamentalists derive two basic principles of separation. First, Christians are to take note of persons whose ideas or actions trouble and challenge the faithful. Thus it is a Christian's formal responsibility to identify clearly and publicly those who have strayed into apostasy and so endanger the fellowship. The fundamentalist penchant for launching vigorous *ad hominem* attacks on reputed apostates is therefore not seen as personal pettiness but as obedience to a biblical mandate. Second, Christians are to "avoid them," that is, to shun false Christians and infidels, withdrawing from all contact with them.[7]

In addition to its biblical soundness, the doctrine of separation is understood by fundamentalists as an essential safeguard against doctrinal impurity. Tolerance, love, unity, inclusivity—these are faulty liberal principles that undermine the principle of biblical truth, which alone can provide the real Christian unity of which the gospel speaks. The strong fundamentalist stance against the ecumenical movement, especially in its conciliar forms, such as the National and World Councils of Churches, is a function of this overriding concern for doctrinal purity. Moreover, without an understanding of the church as an objectively real institution founded by God, fundamentalists have no warrant for seeking unity among believers whose very church membership is predicated upon their unwillingness to compromise doctrinal standards.

The insistence on right doctrine as the center of Christian unity also helps explain why fundamentalists have typically been hostile to the charismatic movement and even to pentecostalism, despite the fact that many members of the two latter groups share basic beliefs that are essentially fundamentalist. Not only do the charismatic and pentecostal emphases on healing, prophecy, miracles, and various gifts of the Spirit contradict dispensationalist views about the present age, but, worse still, charismatics tend to believe that "doctrine divides, love unites." Undoubtedly, writes moderate fundamentalist Edward Dobson, "the charismatic movement has done more to de-emphasize doctrinal differences among varying Christian groups than any other religious movement in the twentieth century."[8] This, naturally, is of serious concern to those who fear the wholesale undermining of truth when doctrine is disregarded.

Most recently, what has been called "secondary separation" has caused bitter dissension among fundamentalists themselves. The basic controversy concerns the appropriateness of separating from erring or weak Christians, that is, from persons who are clearly not infidels, whose infractions are relatively minor and external. But this in turn raises other questions. How separate is "separate"? How sinful must a person's sin be before he or she is avoided? And how thoroughly is "avoidance" to be defined? Does it have to do with sharing dinner as well as sharing church services? Some, like Bob Jones, Jr., have argued that "we must separate not only from avowed unbelief, but also from those who help *promote* unbelief" actively or by association, including, for example, publishers or editors who print articles by suspected infidels.[9] In other words, tolerance of believers who are tolerant of unbelievers is sinful. Other fundamentalists, however, argue that the Bible is clear only in its witness for separation from infidels; preoccupation with degrees of separation can lead to an impossible and self-defeating isolationism.

The Electronic Church

A logical outgrowth of the conservative understanding of the church, with its individualistic, privatized gospel, is "televangelism," or the electronic church. As Charles Grandison Finney's "new measures" for producing revivals were an innovation in the midnineteenth century, so televangelism in the late twentieth century is a genuinely innovative phenomenon that brings new meaning to the acts of preaching, worship, and evangelism. And although electronic magic is no less available to liberals, ironically it has been the conservatively religious who have pioneered in state-of-the-art programming. While liberals have held back, embarrassed perhaps by the gimmickry and glitz of religious show business, conservatives have embraced technological advances that have provided them with the electronic equivalent of a worldwide revival tent.

And they have been enormously successful. Today, with the exception of local programming and occasional specials, virtually all prime-time religious television broadcasting is controlled by conservatives. The names and affiliations of the best-known religious media personalities read like a *Who's Who* of conservative Christianity. Until their much-publicized personal scandals in 1987 and 1988, Jim Bakker and Jimmy Swaggart were both pentecostal in their orientation, with Swaggart a member of the Assemblies of God. Pat Robertson is Southern Baptist; Oral Roberts is from a Pentecostal-Holiness background; Jerry Falwell is independent Baptist; and Robert Schuller is a member of the evangelical Reformed Church in America. All of these men are skilled performers and businessmen as well as preachers. They head (or once did) multi-million dollar industries that involve mass mailings, publishing enterprises, and other subsidiary operations as well as broadcasting. Although studies have been conflicting and inconclusive about the numbers and kinds of viewers they attract, it is clear that these evangelists wield significant influence and generate strong loyalties among their constituencies.

Like the earlier revival meetings of Charles Finney, Dwight Moody, Gipsy Smith, and others, televangelism has generated heated criticism and for many of the same reasons. Mainline Christians especially, troubled by what they perceive to be the simplistic messages and Hollywood trappings of much religious broadcasting, have been quick to list the liabilities of this "new revivalism." It is contrived and manipulative, designed to stir emotions and produce a fast decision for Christ, but it provides no mechanism, they believe, for subsequent nurturing in the faith. It creates spectators and not participants in the worship experience. It offers a truncated evangelistic message, scaled down and simplified for the small screen. It does not teach but offers testimonials. Televangelists themselves are overly preoccupied with money, and they can collect it more easily (thanks to modern technology and improved techniques for mass mailing) by creating the illusion of personalized and individualized "services" to viewers. Unlike local pastors, who have deacons and trustees and judicatories to keep them honest, televangelists are accountable to no one, except perhaps the Internal Revenue Service, and thus they are peculiarly susceptible to the delusions and corruptions of unfettered power.

Undoubtedly the most frequent and serious criticism of the electronic church has to do with its relationship to the whole body of Christ. Televangelism, mainline critics argue, provides little incentive for viewers to join or support a congregation. Thus it serves to replace rather than to augment the local church. Episcopalian John L. Kater, Jr., expresses typical sentiments: "What the preachers of the electronic church proclaim is a distorted Christianity which suggests that we no longer need the church-in-the-flesh. . . . Just as God's presence in the world required a body of flesh and blood, the church has no meaning or identity unless it has a body. The illusory church of the media can offer neither sacramental communion nor the communion of shared life. . . . The disembodied television church is powerless to witness to society."[10] For mainline Christians the real problem with the electronic church is that it is not church at all but an "illusory" substitute that can never share real fulness of life with a broken, needy world.

It is not hard to see the source of conflict here. From the perspective of conservative ecclesiology, televangelism is not an abdication of churchly responsibility nor a departure from orthodoxy. Indeed the very things to which Kater refers (the "church-in-the-flesh," the sacraments) are things that are of minimal importance to many conservatives. They believe that the church exists for and because of individual believers and that its primary purpose, the goal of missions and ministry, is to bring new converts to Christ and encourage the faithful in their commitment to him. Its purpose is emphatically not to build up and maintain an institution. What mainline critics are really attacking is not televangelism, but conservative ecclesiology itself.

This very crucial difference is one reason that conservatives have embraced the electronic media and mainline Christians have not. As every Madison Avenue huckster knows, the small screen is a remarkably persuasive medium, seemingly personal, intimate, private, yet presenting figures that seem larger than life. What better vehicle, then, for persuading people to accept Christ? It is true that some studies have indicated that substantial numbers of those who watch religious programming are already committed Christians; relatively few are actually converted by the televangelists' preaching. But this is no different from the average local church service, in which a conservative pastor may preach a fervently evangelistic message to a congregation, most of whose members consider themselves to be born again. Precisely because the logic of conservative belief demands constant watchfulness over one's own behavior, constant reminders of the necessity of walking in an upright way, in a word, constant revival, it is important for conservatives to hear the basic gospel message repeated again and again. *And* watchfulness is important in order to weed out the nominal Christians who have strayed in amongst the flock. In this context it is no accident, as the words of the familiar evangelical hymn, "I Love to Tell the Story," declare, that those who know the gospel story best "seem hungering and thirsting to hear it like the rest." Just as today's local revivals often take place over a summer week or two in the midst of an already committed faith community, so religious television programming is logically directed at the converted as well as the unconverted. For conservatives, including many evangelically inclined members of the mainline, televangelism serves, at least theoretically, as a source of reaffirmation, renewal, and strengthening of faith.

Sacraments and Ministry

In the mainline churches it is the sacraments (baptism and the Lord's Supper, or eucharist) that offer renewal, strengthening, and refreshment for the professing Christian. Baptism, as discussed earlier, is the initial means by which mainline Christians understand themselves to be united with Christ and one another. It involves both divine initiative, as God freely bestows grace on individual believers, and human response, as a voluntary rite of commitment to God. Baptized persons are freed from bondage to sin, and, identified thereby with Christ's death, are raised with him to new life in both the present and the future. While baptism is believed to be fully effective as a means of grace, "the necessity of faith for the reception of the salvation embodied and set forth is acknowledged by all churches."[12]

Like conservatives, liberal Christians believe that their faith must constantly be reaffirmed. For mainline traditions, however, "the most obvious form of such reaffirmation is the celebration of the eucharist." In the eating of bread and the drinking of wine, Christ grants communion with himself and offers each baptized Christian assurance of forgiveness and the promise of everlasting life. In this periodic act of sharing and reconciliation, Christians are united with one another across boundaries of space and time. And as participants in the Supper, men and women are called to participate in the "ongoing restoration of the world's situation and the human condition," just as Christ himself lived in solidarity with the needy and the outcast.

Christians in both Protestant and Roman Catholic traditions have long debated the nature of Christ's specific involvement with the elements of bread and wine, speculating how these do or do not change their essential nature in the rite itself. The debates have by no means been finally resolved. Yet today's ecumenical convergence points toward a common conviction that the affirmation of Christ's "real, living and active presence in the eucharist" is more important than is the precise determination of how that presence is effected. There is agreement that Christ's real presence (however this is understood) in the sacraments is able to effect genuine, objective transformation in people who receive them. The sacraments are, in other words, means, or channels, of grace, agents of the effects they bring about.

To this "objective" view of the sacraments most conservatives are strongly opposed.[13] They argue that such a viewpoint undermines the supreme importance of a believer's own commitment and decision for the faith; and that taken to its logical conclusion it may even suggest that through the sacraments grace can be imparted in the absence of any faith at all. The practice of infant baptism, dominant (though by no means universal) in the mainline churches, seems to lend credence to this assumption, because its efficacy is dependent upon the faith of the parents and the gathered community, rather than upon that of the child.

Not surprisingly, then, conservatives tend to de-emphasize the sacraments. They are more casual about the particulars of celebration than are their mainline counterparts, and they have generally devoted little attention to either baptismal or eucharistic theology. A few groups eliminate the sacraments entirely, believing that they are part of an earlier dispensation. Others choose not to use the word *sacrament* because of its historic meaning; instead they substitute *ordinance*, which suggests simply a prescribed ceremony or practice. In some evangelical and pentecostal traditions, footwashing is an ordinance of equal importance to the Lord's Supper and is usually celebrated immediately after the latter rite.

In general, conservatives share a "memorial" view of the Lord's Supper. Christ is not objectively present "in, around, and under" the elements, although he is subjectively present in the minds and hearts of believers as they reenact and remember his last supper with the apostles. Believers do not expect to be changed by participating in either baptism or the Lord's Supper, for change has already been initiated in the process of conversion. Rather, their participation is a personal testimony to the congregation that they are among the faithful.

Almost without exception, conservative fellowships baptize adult believers by immersion, with pentecostal and charismatic traditions explicitly distinguishing this "water baptism" from the "Spirit baptism" that characterizes their traditions. It is not uncommon for some groups to insist on rebaptism if a believer has been baptized as an infant or sprinkled as an adult in another fellowship. Occasionally rebaptism is recommended if a converted person backslides but repents and returns to the faith. The logic of rebaptism, of course, is wholly dependent upon a testimonial understanding of the rite. For mainline Christians rebaptism is tantamount to the suggestion that Christ's own power is not efficacious.

In both mainline and conservative fellowships, it is generally a duly ordained minister who, as representative of both Christ and the church or congregation, celebrates the ordinances or sacramental rites. But in the area of ministry conservative groups share a certain unstudied ambiguity, perhaps in part because the Bible itself is not entirely clear about what ministry is or what sort of persons ministers might be. Two historical models of ministry are identifiable. The first is that of the minister as a leader with special gifts, or charisms. In early New Testament times, ministry was indistinguishable from the servant life and the mission of Jesus Christ himself. All Spirit-filled followers of Jesus were ministers; and ministry, according to Paul, was understood to involve a variety of personal gifts and abilities, each of them divinely inspired and necessary for the upbuilding of the church. Because they are equal before God, Paul seems to say, all follower-ministers are equal among themselves.[14] In those conservative traditions that have stressed the varieties of personal gifts, particularly pentecostalism and historic evangelicalism, the model of minister as leader with special gifts for service has predominated, with the gifts themselves, rather than formal theological education, serving as primary validation for the ministerial call. In these Spirit-centered traditions, women and minorities have often taken a more active role in ministry, although the institutionalization of such groups has tended eventually to reproduce the white, male-dominated clergy of the surrounding ecclesial culture.

A second and more common model is that of the minister as a spiritually superior functionary. The importance of the functions of leadership, communication, and instruction in the expanding young Christian church—and the resulting prestige of the functionaries who carried them out—eventually produced what has been called "two-order Christianity," a faith of leaders and of the led, of stratified ministerial and lay roles. In time, an initial acknowledgment of different roles and gifts evolved into the acknowledgment of differences in personal status or being, evidenced by those same roles and gifts. Thus the leadership of the church came gradually to be understood as both functionally and spiritually distinct from the larger body of believers.

In conservative churches today, emphasis on the Christian life encourages, at the formal level, a "low" view of ministry, with an accompanying emphasis on the priesthood of all believers. Because conservatives tend to value personal piety and spiritual gifts above theological education, their clergy and laity may not be significantly differentiated by knowledge and "professional" skills. Unlike some mainline Christians, moreover, conservatives do not identify the ordained ministry in its sacramental role as a mark of the true church. Nevertheless, ministers, especially those with rhetorical gifts, may be vested with enormous power and authority by their flocks, whether the latter are in the pews or in front of their television sets. Ministers are understood to be spiritual exemplars, living and imitatable models of true faithfulness. Even a backsliding minister offers a worthy model, if in public witness he (much more rarely, she) illustrates the path of repentance and humility that most Christians sooner or later will have to walk for their souls' sake.

Missions and Mission

"Go therefore and make disciples of all nations [Matt. 28:19]." In commissioning his disciples, Jesus ensured that the church would be directly involved in the whole world. But what exactly does making disciples involve? What is the mission of the church?

The first settlers and explorers in the New World almost invariably stated their intention to "bring the gospel to the American savages" as one reason for their transatlantic migration. But the difficulties of community building in a wilderness and the problems of alien languages and life-styles contributed to the early failure of their hopes. Nearly two hundred years passed before American Protestants were to engage in mission activity on any significant scale.

At the beginning of the nineteenth century, the second Great Awakening and the opening of the West combined to rekindle evangelistic vision. By midcentury, new Protestant zeal for missions resulted in the founding of the interdenominational American Board of Commissioners for Foreign Missions and the American Home Missionary Society. Missionaries were dispatched not only to the American frontier but around the world. Their goal was simple, grand, and sincerely held: to evangelize the world, to bring the gospel to people who had not heard it, and to bring those hearers to Christ.

After the Civil War, missionary activity accelerated, due in part to the leadership of evangelist Dwight L. Moody and the YMCA movement among young college-age students. But after the turn of the century the missionary agenda came under increasing attack. Presbyterian Joseph E. McAfee summarized the new perspective.

> If the missionary maintains that the individualistic method is ultimate, and represents an individualistic scheme of salvation as final and complete, he runs counter to approved world tendencies and repudiates a social theory which schools of thought in all civilized lands are successfully establishing.[15]

New and complex problems at home, caused by urban poverty, labor and economic problems, illiteracy, and alienation, presented challenges for which the old solutions of revival and soul-saving seemed to many an inadequate response. At the same time, foreign missions came under fire for their paternalistic methods, as well as for the "cultural imperialism" that underlay much of their programming.[16]

After World War I, the Protestant churches embraced McAfee's conclusions, altering their mission agendas to include more than a narrowly defined program of evangelism. But this drift away from a traditional understanding of missions served to widen the already existing gap between liberals and conservatives, and thus the "missions question" became one more corrosive ingredient in the fundamentalist-modernist controversy of the time.

Today both conservative and mainline churches have developed more sophisticated mechanisms for mission activity, and both groups are aware of the long-term effects, both positive and negative, of nineteenth-century missions. Increasingly "indigenization," that is, the development of a church and social leadership that emerges out of a people's own context, is the common goal of mission work. Nevertheless, there remains a basic difference, often illustrated by the continuing use of the traditional word *missions* by conservatives and of *mission* by mainline Protestants. Far more liberals than conservatives have embraced the idea that authentic mission involves commitment to social change as well as to religious change. In general liberals promote not only evangelism but also programs for global awareness, improved living conditions, liberation from oppressive governmental systems, economic justice, and peace. For liberals it is axiomatic that evil is often systemic, embedded in the very fabric and structures of society. Real mission demands that Christians work to effect positive social change in all arenas of life, for the gospel is not only words but actions.

Although conservatives too provide direct action programming through a variety of denominational and interdenominational mission agencies, it is clear that evangelism itself remains the basic and primary goal of this work. It is God who effects meaningful change through changed hearts and lives; thus it is the church's responsibility to provide the means and forum for the hearing of God's transforming word. Unquestionably programs founded on this understanding have had significant social as well as personal effects. For example, pentecostal David Wilkerson's well-known Teen Challenge ministry (now a global program) has had important consequences in the world of New York's youthful street and drug culture. Wilkerson and other conservative leaders, however, continue to approach such problems from the individualistic and evangelistic perspectives that characterized the Protestant churches of the last century. And they argue that history suggests the evangelistic method is *more* effective in promoting real change than are the modern, social scientific approaches of the liberal churches.

Chapter 5

The Church and Society

What is the appropriate relationship of the Christian church to its historical and social context? Should Christians embrace God's good creation, actively seeking to effect change and growth within it? Or should they withdraw from the sinful world to establish a community of holy and sanctified believers, living in right relationship to God and awaiting a divinely transformed future? These have long been vexing questions for which Christians have discovered many answers but little agreement.

Categories of Christian Response to Society

Historically, the often conflicting responses of the church to the world have been analyzed in a variety of ways. Early in the twentieth century, Ernst Troeltsch described two dominant kinds of religious groups in his famous "church-sect" typology. Sect-type bodies, according to Troeltsch, respond to the culture in which they reside mainly by withdrawal and rejection. Their intent is to create pure communities of believers, separated from secular society and its corruptions. Underlying this response is the belief that Christ as Lord is to be understood primarily as the judge of the purity of his gathered flock. Church-type groups, on the other hand, are more open and responsive to their host culture. They perceive church and society as essentially interconnected, rather than radically distinct. From this perspective, Christ is understood primarily as the source of renewal and redemption for both church and world. Although today many scholars consider them to be overly simplified and general, Troeltsch's categories still provide helpful interpretive guidelines. Conservative Christian groups, for example, more nearly fit the sect-type, whereas mainline groups may logically be described as church-type.

One scholar deeply influenced by Troeltsch and his work is H. Richard Niebuhr, whose five-part typology built on and augmented Troeltsch's own. Niebuhr identified five categories that describe different Christian perceptions of Jesus' relationship to society. Of these, the first, fourth, and last are perhaps most representative of conservative groups; mainline churches may be identified with all but the first, but especially with the second and frequently with the final category. "Christ against culture" describes an essentially anticultural stance in which the claims of society on individual Christians are utterly rejected in the name of higher loyalty to Christ. "Christ of culture" denotes a position in which church and world, religious and secular behavior are understood as essentially conterminous. Loyalty to Jesus thus "leads to active participation in every cultural work," as well as to the accommodation of religious practice to cultural norms. "Christ above culture" is a centrist position that values both church and world, without attempting either to separate them or to link them. The position of "Christ and culture in paradox" views the human situation dualistically: while sin makes Christ's lordship over society problematic, nevertheless, Christians must live in a culture even as they follow rules for life that are independent of that culture. The final category, "Christ the transformer of culture," represents the "conversionist" affirmation that, in spite of the sin embedded in human structures and institutions, all life is under God's sovereignty; thus "the Christian must carry on cultural work in obedience to the Lord" in the hope of effecting positive change. [1]

This multiplicity of Christian responses to society and culture is a function of many variables, including the historical realities of wealth and poverty, oppression and dominance, majority and minority, war and peace, that have impacted the church in different times and places. One common theological variable, however, is the biblical concept of the kingdom of God. In its presentation of the idea of the kingdom, the New Testament offers Christians a kind of paradox. A central motif in the four Gospels is that in Jesus Christ God's kingdom has come; God's sovereignty

over world and church has been firmly established. Yet elsewhere—
for example, in the apocalyptic predictions in the Revelation to
John—the kingdom seems to be a future event, a reality about to
break in but not yet consummated. Because of this apparent
ambiguity, Christians have typically understood the kingdom to
exist in a kind of tension. It is both already here and not yet. It
has, in a mysterious way, manifested itself in the present, but its
perfected work remains a future expectation and hope.

In practice, however, Christians have rarely maintained this
balanced understanding. Instead they have tended to stress one
side of the equation or the other. Those who have emphasized the
present, here-and-now dimensions of the kingdom have often
attempted enthusiastically to transform the social order in the
name of God's already established leadership. Many of America's
nineteenth-century evangelicals, for instance, understood themselves to be in a kind of partnership with God, their benevolent
activities hastening the completion of God's work by bringing
history into conformity with the divine will. From this perspective,
history itself has redemptive significance. It is the stage on which
the drama of grace, already begun, will draw eventually to its
triumphant close.

Those who understand the kingdom primarily as imminent, or
not yet, tend to have a more pessimistic view of history. For these
Christians history is not the scene of God's redemptive activity; it
is, rather, the context for the struggle, sin, and suffering that must
inevitably precede God's final breaking in. At that future time all
history and humankind will be judged and the kingdom inaugu-
rated with the creation of a "new heaven and a new earth."

Not all conservative or mainline Christians have clearly articulated doctrines of the kingdom or formally expressed understandings of Christ's relationship to culture. Yet underlying their
orientations toward society are discernible theological beliefs about
the nature of the kingdom and the world. Among mainline
Christians, the old "evolutionary optimism" of the nineteenth
century has now virtually disappeared. No longer do people
anticipate that the positive, progressive movement of history will
inevitably bring about the consummation of God's plan for the
world. Nevertheless, the prevailing mainline emphasis on the

immanent, or indwelling, reality of God's kingdom in our midst provides warrant for active involvement in programs for social transformation.

Conservatives, on the other hand, more often focus on the breaking in of a radically new and different reality at some unknown future moment. Often this perspective is linked with a premillennial understanding of Christ's second coming, with its characteristic assumptions about the imminent and prior reign of Antichrist and the collapse of human institutions. Consequently, some conservatives view the present as a time of trouble and trial, in which the best they can hope for is the continued faithfulness of God's people as they live out the world's dark final days. Others— especially those who view America as a "new Israel," a nation in covenant with God—couple this eschatological hope with a harsh judgment of the nation's present moral and spiritual state. Because they believe that America's collective behavior is both a seal and a condition of God's continued special blessing, they may be ex- tremely vocal and politically active in their attempt to regulate national behavior.

In contrast to these primarily evangelical or fundamentalist viewpoints, pentecostals and charismatics typically insist that the gifts of the Spirit that characterize their traditions are themselves indications of a new reality. They are "not just a historical sign of the coming of the new age but also the opening of the era of the Spirit in which the power of the kingdom is to be continuously and presently manifested."[2] For these two groups, the contemporary outpouring of the Spirit, evidenced in healings, signs and wonders, and other blessings, is joyfully accepted as an indication that the world is in its last days. Social involvement, therefore, is likely to be identified primarily with an exuberant and empowered evan- gelism. Matthew reveals this anticipated scenario clearly: "This gospel of the kingdom will be preached throughout the whole world . . . . and then the end will come [Matt. 24:14]."

The Rise of the Evangelical Right

More than anything else it is the appearance of the so-called Evangelical Right (or New Christian Right or Religious Right)[3] that has taken mainline Christians and others by surprise. After nearly fifty years of voluntary absence from the political scene, conservative Christians seemed to have emerged almost overnight in the early 1970s as a new political and social force, ready to translate their convictions into concrete policies and programs. Within a decade, conservatives had outstripped liberals in their active involvement, creating political action groups, lobbying, and marshaling vast sums of money to underwrite conservatively supported legislation.

Despite the surprise they generated, however, conservatives were in fact reclaiming a much older heritage of social engagement. As previous chapters indicate, during the nineteenth century, evangelical Christians were directly involved in a host of secular and sacred causes, including temperance, feminism, women's suffrage, urban reform, missions, labor relations, education, and (albeit tardily) the abolition of slavery. Their goal was nothing less than the creation of a thoroughgoing Christian commonwealth, a nation with a "free, literate, industrious, honest, law-abiding religious population."[4] For many, these goals were undergirded by the belief (a formative part of America's self-perception since the time of the Puritans) that God was making this nation a special instrument, like Israel, for the completion of a divine plan. Even the tragedy of the Civil War, which split several major denominations along sectional lines, altered the vision only slightly. For both sides the Civil War was a holy war; and, for Northerners at least, it was linked to the powerful vision of Christ's righteous kingdom, familiarly expressed in Julia Ward Howe's famous "Battle Hymn of the Republic":

> In the beauty of the lilies Christ was born across the sea,
> With a glory in his bosom that transfigures you and me.
> As he died to make men holy, let us die to make men free.
> While God is marching on.

Inevitably the Civil War engendered disillusionment and reaction among Christians and non-Christians alike. Yet even these feelings were tempered by an overriding confidence and hopefulness among many, bolstered by the apparent stability of American institutions and the social advances that had been made under the influence of Christianity, including, ironically, the abolition of slavery itself. Expanding missionary activity, interdenominational cooperation, and a pervasive sense of the moral superiority of American culture brought Protestants into the twentieth century in a general mood of optimism. The organization of the Federal Council of Churches of Christ in America in 1908, a coalition of nearly thirty fellowships, reflected the broad consensus that its task was to evangelize the world. When the First World War intervened shortly thereafter, these groups viewed the hostilities as an opportunity, a "Great Crusade" that could lead ultimately to the fulfillment of the vision of world Christianity.

But all this was to change, and change rapidly, in the years after the war. Not one but several factors combined to produce a radically altered situation characterized by disillusionment and divisiveness. The natural letdown after the "war to end all wars" was one decisive factor. Another was the waning authority of the churches themselves in an era of shifting population and cultural, racial, and ethnic diversity. The twilight of rural America and the rise of vast, sprawling urban complexes produced new problems for which old solutions and visions now appeared inadequate and anachronistic. Black Americans, their plight virtually disregarded even by proponents of the new Social Gospel, raised critical voices against the churches that had supported their emancipation and then failed entirely to deal with the "race problem" that had resulted. Above all, new developments in science and technology undercut long-cherished, familiar, and comforting patterns of religious belief.

One significant result of this social and intellectual turmoil was what David O. Moberg has called "the great reversal": the withdrawal, hastened by the humiliating Scopes trial, of evangelical Protestants, pentecostals, and fundamentalists from active involvement in social issues.[5] Between roughly 1930 and the mid-1970s, conservative Christianity "institutionalized its suspicion of ecumenism and the social gospel," focusing its collective attention on attacking personal sins instead of public corruption.[6]

Some, however, were from the outset uncomfortable with this evangelical withdrawal, and as far back as 1947 alternative voices began again to speak out. One of the most influential of these was Carl F. H. Henry, whose widely read book *The Uneasy Conscience of Modern Fundamentalism* in that year called for a reformation in the passive social attitudes of conservatives. "The redemptive message has applications for all of life," warned Henry. "A truncated life results from a truncated message."[7] The gradual development of both local and international cooperative ministries over the next two decades signaled a cautious renewal of social concern among some evangelicals. By 1976, evangelical activity and visibility had so increased that, in a much-touted cover story, *Newsweek* magazine declared it "The Year of the Evangelical." But it was not until the founding of Jerry Falwell's politically aggressive Moral Majority in June 1979 that fundamentalists formally emerged alongside evangelicals as an active, assertive, and—most startling to liberals—influential social and political force. Assessments vary as to the effectiveness of the Moral Majority in changing minds and garnering votes. But there can be no doubt that during the ten years of its existence the organization brilliantly focused attention on the views of its long-silent constituency, as well as on conservative Christianity in general.[8]

The high visibility profile and aggressive style of the Moral Majority from its beginning often served to symbolize the social agenda of the whole New Christian Right for outsiders. But like conservatives themselves, this agenda is not all of a piece. Although many contemporary conservatives share a renewed commitment to political and social engagement, their commitment takes a number of very different forms and reflects a variety of theological understandings. What virtually all conservatives have in common, however, despite their very different and even conflicting social strategies or lack of them, is the high priority they place on evangelism as a means for social reformation. Even when structural change is advocated or direct action counseled, these are not separable from an overriding concern for personal renewal and regeneration. Indeed, the general conservative critique of mainline social activism (especially as the latter is represented in the ecumenical movement)[9] is not only a negative response to liberal strategies and solutions, but represents the profound conviction that liberals have inverted their priorities. For, say conservatives, it is God's transforming presence in the lives of individual believers that offers the most important foundation for permanent change.

Today at least four different perspectives on social reformation and responsibility may be identified among conservatives.[10] First,

despite the extraordinary publicity that evangelical and fundamentalist activism received during the 1980s, many conservative
Christians remain convinced that the primary task for Christianity
is not direct social involvement at all. Rather it is, as it has always
been, evangelism, bringing the gospel message to a needy world,
for salvation is the one realistic hope for reformation. Christians
who embrace this perspective stress the need for personal and
societal renewal through conversion and the importance of an
informed citizenry that bases its political choices on sound biblical
principles. Like their nineteenth-century forebears, they are sen-
sitive to the pain, suffering, and ignorance around them; but they
are much more likely to respond to these problems by proposing
ministries of benevolence and spiritual renewal than by engaging
in direct action for change. In general, these Christians do not
participate in sustained social analysis and are unlikely to devote
much attention to the problem of systemic evil in the world.

A second perspective, perhaps best represented by the widely
read evangelical magazine *Christianity Today,* is explicitly concerned with a broad range of social, political, and moral issues
(though perhaps especially with the latter category). Christians in
this group may be knowledgeably critical of American society and
institutions, both in their personal and political dimensions. They
are not unaware of systemic problems. Nevertheless, their basic
social stance is one of ecclesial noninvolvement. While responsible
social criticism and the encouragement of specific solutions are
understood to be appropriate for the churches (as are traditional
programs of benevolence) active, participatory social reform is
more appropriately left to individual initiative. Moreover, although
solutions to social problems certainly should be pursued, they are
not, in the end, effective ways to respond to the world's pain and
alienation. Rather, turning to Jesus Christ and his principles, to
personal belief and holiness, can provide the only stable and sure
hope for social reformation.

A third conservative perspective shares with the liberal mainline
a thoroughgoing, occasionally radical, critique of contemporary
American society (and often a critique of other conservatives).
Christians in this group—for the most part they are "new evangelicals" who represent a small but growing minority voice within
the conservative spectrum—share a social ethic that calls for

concrete political engagement in matters relating to both individual and systemic sin. They are advocates of a social agenda that
goes beyond mere benevolence. Many of them are vitally concerned with the active promotion of justice and peace. While they
believe that only God can bring about the kingdom, their hope in
God's promises imbues with meaning specific programs for renewal
and change.

Within this general grouping is an even smaller but prolific core
of radical social critics, best exemplified by Jim Wallis and the
well-known Sojourners community, but also represented in the
work of Mennonite John Howard Yoder and the late Baptist
liberation theologian Orlando Costas. For these believers, the
church is called to witness daily to the sinful systems of the world.
But this cannot be accomplished through direct political activity to
effect change, because such involvement invariably involves unacceptable compromise with the systems themselves. Instead, the
church's best strategy must be intentionally to withdraw from the
structures of society in order to create new, faithful, and just
communities. By standing outside the existing order, these communities hope in effect to subvert the status quo by their own
countercultural witness.

A final perspective includes supporters of the now-disbanded
Moral Majority and those with similar views about the present
precarious state of the nation and world. Probably a majority of
moderate fundamentalists and many evangelicals fall into this
perceptual category, although by no means are all of them activists.
Unlike persons in the first three categories, these believers can
often be trenchant critics of what they perceive to be a dangerously
permissive American society. Thus they support legislation that
would limit (among other things) abortion on demand, drug use,
sexual permissiveness, homosexuality, pornography, and secular
humanism. They are vocally opposed to Communism because it is
atheistic, to the peace movement because it threatens to undermine American hegemony in the world, and to feminism because
it undercuts the traditional family. These Christians tend to accept
the American capitalist system uncritically. Many of them attribute to the nation a special, God-given calling and destiny, a
belief that lends particular urgency to their political activity on
behalf of favored causes. Their legislative concerns, however, often

(though not exclusively) focus on matters of individual morality rather than on systemic issues such as the environment, human rights, or economic justice. It is a mark of the influence of this group that its chief spokespersons in both the political and the ecclesial world are household names even in non-Christian communities: Jerry Falwell, Carl McIntire, Jesse Helms, Pat Robertson, Ronald Reagan.[11]

Why have these persons and the movement they represent engendered so much sustained public attention? Historian Grant Wacker argues that what is generally assumed to be widespread evangelical growth is really not the growth of "evangelicalism, conceived as a religious and theological movement, but rather [of] a segment within Evangelicalism defined by its allegiance to a cluster of values derived from Victorian middle-class society." This "smaller, more overtly politicized segment" of conservative Christianity Wacker identifies as the "Evangelical Right," and the goal it seeks is a biblically centered "Christian Civilization." Distinguishing contemporary right-wing evangelicalism from more traditional positions, Wacker argues that "the Evangelical non-Right . . . is not measurably stronger now than it was ten or twenty or even fifty years ago." In other words, it is the group for which the Moral Majority has provided real and symbolic political cohesiveness that represents the growing edge of conservative Christianity itself.

Several specific viewpoints characterize this emerging Evangelical Right: the insistence that moral absolutes exist and that they transcend specific historical circumstances; the assumption that "for every moral question there is one and only one morally correct answer"; the conviction that moral absolutes must provide the cornerstones for the laws that order American society; the sure knowledge that these absolutes are evidenced in nature and explicitly revealed in the Bible. The Evangelical Right is vehemently opposed to pluralism and to libertarianism, to the liberal media, to educational institutions that promote relativism and the clinically impartial study of traditional beliefs, and, above all, to secular humanism, which they believe subtly and perniciously undercuts the spiritual fiber of the nation.[12]

Although not all interpreters agree that only this segment of conservative Christianity has experienced significant growth during recent decades, it is clear that the Evangelical Right and its distinctive beliefs have, not without reason, virtually defined the popular understanding of politicized conservative Christianity. Consequently, these beliefs—an attitude toward America that borrows Old Testament themes of covenant and chosenness from New England Puritanism, a negative, even alarmist, assessment of the present, and a comprehensive political agenda for solving the ills of the nation—all merit closer examination.

It was John Winthrop, first governor of Massachusetts Bay, who best articulated the Puritans' hopes for their experimental New World colony. It was to be a "city upon a hill," a Christian commonwealth so exemplary that the whole world (and especially England) would see it and seek to imitate it. The Puritans' reading of the scriptures, particularly the Old Testament, convinced them that their own settlement was truly a "new Israel"; they themselves were God's chosen people. Convinced that God was covenanting with them to help bring about a divine plan for all the nations, the Puritans habitually interpreted the various events of their common life as signs of God's wrath, pleasure, or warning. In their providential worldview, divine causality reigned; there was no room for chance. Thus the Puritans walked a fine line between hope and anxiety, self-aggrandizement and self-recrimination. They knew well that God's special blessings could swiftly be turned around to bitter punishment if their half of the covenant remained unfulfilled.

Although the Puritans' holy experiment was moribund by 1690 and virtually extinct by the time of the first Great Awakening, their vision of a genuinely new and blessed world in America remained remarkably viable through generations of immigrants, war, and the steady secularization of American society. Thus Jerry Falwell could say without embarrassment in 1980:

> I am convinced that the real crisis in America is a moral crisis which supersedes our economic, our military, our energy crises. I am convinced that what Solomon said in the Proverbs, thirty-five hundred years ago, is the key to our survival. He said, and I paraphrase, living by God's principles promotes a nation to greatness. Violating God's principles brings a nation to shame. The last 20 to 30 years we have

suffered shame and of late, international embarrassment
because we have been violating God's principles.[13]

Today some observers, like Falwell himself, downplay the interpretation of America's history and purpose as a sacred calling in favor
of more generalized principles about God and governance. Others
take for granted that from the beginning God has had a special
interest in America. But so thoroughgoing is a sense of the nation's
uniqueness that this theme is present in a variety of forms in
virtually every stratum of American Christianity. Writes sociologist
Robert Bellah in a well-known essay: "The obligation, both
collective and individual, to carry out God's will on earth . . . was
the motivating spirit of those who founded America, and it has
been present in every generation since."[14]

In this respect, of course, the assumption of a unique God-given
national destiny does not distinguish conservatives in the Evangelical Right from millions of other Americans. What is distinctive, however, is the yoking of the idea of national destiny with
that of divine wrath and judgment, and the need for a concrete
program of Christian response. Like their Puritan forebears,
Falwell and his colleagues in this broadbased group see all around
them the signs of America's apostasy and God's angry response.
The crisis of AIDS, the moral laxity of youth, the disintegration of
family life and the rising divorce rate, the spread of worldwide
Communism and socialism, the teaching of what conservatives
perceive as value-free education in America's school systems—all
these are ominous signs of the times. But perhaps the two areas
that have generated the most sustained concern within the Evangelical Right are those of secular humanism and the beleaguered
"traditional family."

Humanism, in the sense of a high valuation of humanity's
cultural achievements and a strong faith in the basic goodness and
competence of women and men, is no new phenomenon. In one
form or another it has been present throughout America's common
life and institutions from the time of the nation's founding. It can
be discerned even today in the determined individualism of conservative Christianity itself.[15] But the secular humanism about
which the Evangelical Right is vitally concerned is perceived as
less benign, more subtle, and a dangerous phenomenon that

threatens to undercut the very foundations of Christian civilization.[16] In the view of Tim LaHaye (whose extraordinary popular
book *The Battle for the Mind* is a classic exposition of the Evangelical Right's perspective), secular humanism is essentially a
religion that places ultimate faith in humanity as the source of
power and value. It is "man's attempt to solve his problems
independently of God."[17] This "attempt" is more than mere
accident or error. It is intentional, the product of a coherent
alternative value system whose fundamental tenets are atheism,
evolution, amorality, human autonomy, and "one-world socialism."
Its influence is incontrovertibly manifested in, among other things,
the pervasive self-centeredness of twentieth-century Americans,
the belief in evolution and scientific method, internationalism,
and moral relativism.

To this description of humanism and its accompanying litany of
modern woes, the mainline Christian response has been a combination of incredulity and amusement. Some, in fact, have
compared the overblown fear of secular humanism to the famous
"Red Scare" of the mid-1950s. Liberals have argued that, with the
possible exception of a few minor leftist groups with origins in the
radicalism of the 1930s, no formal alliance of secular humanists
exists; no humanist conspiracy to subvert the institutions of public
life has to date been discovered.

Yet the Evangelical Right has a point. Behind all the hyperbole
and alarmist rhetoric are several observations about, and interpretations of, contemporary American life that mainline Christians
have often failed to appreciate. For one thing, the fact that secular
humanism is embodied in no formal organization renders it no less
real or, from a conservative perspective, potentially threatening. If
anything, to conservatives, the very diffuseness and invisibility of
the phenomenon make its effects more subtle and pernicious.
Further, conservatives have correctly observed that, undergirding
the institutions of America's public life, particularly the media and
school systems, is a corpus of shared understandings that do indeed
offer an alternative to traditional Christian beliefs.

What is the nature of this alternative? Most obvious is the
understanding that all values (truth, law, customs, morality) are
socially conditioned. They are not the products of divine law but
of particular times and places, habits and events, and historical

circumstances; they are infinitely changeable. Second is an almost religious reliance on the tools of modern scientific inquiry, perhaps most notably the social and behavioral sciences, for the "impartial" reexamination of our inherited traditions and beliefs. An impartial or agnostic examination of facts, the Evangelical Right maintains, is an impossibility; it is not neutral or value-free at all. It represents the very real value of impartiality concerning God, which is itself a value profoundly antagonistic to the conservative Christian understanding of reality. Yet it is this false neutrality on which America's leaders typically rely for decision making. Finally, in practice these relativized, "value-free" ideas impel our teachers and officials to portray as normative (or at best, as merely different) those lifestyles and behaviors that to conservatives may be aberrant and sinful. Thus, for example, the typical objection of conservatives to public school programming about sex and death does not derive, as some have assumed, from residual sentiments of Victorian prudery. Instead it reveals the well-founded concern that teachers will explain in a morally neutral way matters which to conservatives have vitally important moral content.

A second matter of great significance for the Evangelical Right is the contemporary plight of the American family. It is the Christian family that provides both order in the lives of individual persons and fundamental stability for the nation and its institutions; it is the family that is the primary building-block for America's collective well-being. Although, as mainline critics have often pointed out, the biblical foundation for the belief is scanty at best, many conservatives understand the family as a social structure created and blessed by God for a distinctive divine purpose. Not only is the family (as Paul suggests in, for example, I Corinthians 7:8–9) a hedge against rampant and illicit passions, but it is also the place where good Christian and American values are to be handed down to new generations of godly citizens. Thus the traditional family fulfills both a personal and a societal mission of no little importance.

By *family*, of course, the Evangelical Right means the traditional family unit: a man and woman, united formally by Christian marriage and living in a "hierarchic but equal" relationship in which the husband is primary breadwinner and decision maker and the wife is subordinate and concerned primarily with domestic affairs. To the Right this structure is not a matter of European-American custom but of God's eternal will. "God Almighty created men and women biologically different and with differing needs and roles," claims Jerry Falwell.[18] Many conservatives (even those less politicized than the Evangelical Right) would agree, arguing that because women are the "weaker vessel" they are no less important in God's order of existence. Although the Evangelical Right is generally supportive of equal rights and equal pay for women (the Moral Majority formerly listed equal rights as one of ten "vital issues" for its consideration), it tends to separate the practical issue of equality from the issues of essential (or ontological) human function and role. In this schema, it is not perceived as illogical that Phyllis Schlafly, a highly paid, professional businesswoman who earns more than her husband, spends much of her time away from home, speaking and writing about traditional family values and structures. What is important is that she understand and support God's essential order for humankind, an order in which, regardless of their temporal jobs or activities, men and women are eternally yoked as head and subordinate, just as Christ is the eternal head of the church.

Because the family in this "traditional"[19] sense is so foundational to its entire worldview, the Evangelical Right is actively opposed to all those contemporary developments that threaten it. Chief among these is feminism. Indeed, the Right sees in the feminist movement the root cause of many of the besetting moral sins of America today, for at its heart feminism is nothing if not women's deliberate rejection of their appropriate roles, and by extension, of the Bible that reveals them. Thus the Equal Rights Amendment (which some claimed was defeated largely by organized conservative Christian opposition) had a deeply symbolic as well as very practical import. It represented a profound legal challenge to the authority of the Bible itself, as well as to the concepts of masculinity and femininity that conservatives discover therein.

Secular humanism and issues related to family life are not the only concerns of the Evangelical Right that have political implications. The protection and revitalization of America's capitalist free-enterprise system is of critical importance, as is the maintenance of a strong national defense program. Both serve as a hedge against the spread of international Communism and its atheistic ideology.[20] Support of a free and secure Israel is also a central concern for many. In the prophetic scheme of premillennial dispensationalism, the scriptures clearly indicate that at the end of the age, the restoration of Israel will set in motion the events of the world's final days. The actual establishment of the modern state of Israel in 1948 seems to offer undeniable indication that this program is already underway, and the time for action and repentance short.

In all this, more than a few adherents of the Evangelical Right find themselves on the horns of a dilemma, for if America is, in some ultimate sense, a Christian civilization that is part of God's plan, then these present ills are symptoms not only of human failing but of divine displeasure. On the face of it, their solution is clear and urgent: America must be brought back to God's ways, if necessary through forcible legal measures, so that its temporal health as well as its role in God's salvific scheme may be assured.

Ironically, however, the eschatological implications of premillennialism have historically militated against just this sort of activism. In general, premillennialists have responded to their sense of imminent destruction with spiritual, not political, solutions: Christians should be watchful, prayerful, and, above all, spiritually prepared. What is the purpose, after all, of attempting to effect any sort of social change when the world teeters at the brink of Armageddon? The entry into the political arena of fundamentalists with premillennial and dispensationalist views is logically inconsistent with a theology that looks to the immediate ending of society and politics as we know them.

Nevertheless, premillennialists in the Evangelical Right have justified their support of various political causes in different ways, depending in part on their understanding of the relationship of the church's "rapture" to the time of tribulation.[21] Historian Timothy P. Weber has pointed out that some premillennialists like Jerry Falwell and Hal Lindsey never have demonstrated a convincing connection between their eschatologies, or understanding of the end times, and their right-wing politics. Lindsey (whose 1970 book of prophecies, *The Late Great Planet Earth,* is one of the best-selling volumes of the entire century) does seem to suggest that bringing America back to God's ways "right now" can at least delay the nation's precipitous decline until the rapture; while Falwell "simply wants to put America back the way he thinks it was, to repair its now disintegrating Christian . . . foundations." Others, like post-tribulation survivalist Jim McKeever, emphasize physical preparedness, because Christians will need to develop new habits of self-sufficiency if they are to live through the reign of Antichrist. [22]

To this new flexing of conservative muscle in the political world, mainline Christians have responded with a mixture of anger, incredulity, and occasionally approval. Generalizations about the mainline's own involvement with political activity are somewhat risky. Today some theologically liberal Christians insist that the churches should stay out of politics entirely; others argue that they should keep their membership informed about important political issues but avoid advocating specific solutions. Some denominations, including several Lutheran bodies, have because of their distinctive beliefs generally downplayed active social engagement.

Nevertheless it is true that, from the postmillennial fervor of the nineteenth century to the Social Gospel that prevailed during the first part of this century, many mainline Christians have insisted that human renewal, not only church renewal through evangelism and missions, is a Christian calling. From this perspective, Christian men and women are to be "in but not of" the world, working for human betterment with all the God-given tools at their disposal. These liberal believers have rarely devoted much serious attention to future events such as the tribulation or the rapture, for it is clear to them that the future contains mysteries that only God can affect, whereas in the present Christians themselves can make a tangible difference.

But what if contemporary conservatives also hope to make a difference with their own programs, ones that conflict with the very programs for social renewal that liberals have often supported? Here is the dilemma in which mainline Christians presently find themselves. For if the gospel demands that Christians embody their beliefs in concrete form, then surely it demands the same of all Christians, not only liberal ones.

Chapter 6

The Whole Body of Christ

It has been the purpose of these chapters to offer a series of general descriptive statements about conservative and mainline Christianity for the purpose of mutual understanding, not for any sort of adversarial comparison. Although my own liberal bias may have been evident throughout in language, organization, and choice of material, for the most part I have attempted to present the data impartially. But in these concluding pages I want to risk some prescriptive generalizations—not at all impartial—about what the church needs to become in the context of what it is and has been.

On Becoming a "Both/And" Fellowship

Matthew tells us that when Jesus asked his disciples, "Who do you say that I am?" Simon Peter did not stop to reflect on the meaning of the words he was about to say. He answered very quickly, "You are the Christ, the Child of the living God." And Jesus' own response was quick and approving: "Blessed are you, Simon Bar-Jona! For flesh and blood has not revealed this to you, but God who is in heaven. And I tell you, you are Peter, and on this rock I will build my church [Matt. 16:14–18, passim]."

This encounter was, of course, the beginning of the Christian church. And from the beginning, this brief conversation has raised as many questions for the church as it has answered. The problem, in part, is that it leaves so much unsaid. What does it mean for Jesus to be "Child of God?" If he is the Child of God, how are we to understand his nature or personality—is it divine or human or

77

some sort of hybrid? What should the church look like? Who should lead it in Peter's absence? And why was it that Jesus chose to found his church "on this rock" (in Latin, *petrus*, meaning rock)? Was it because Peter accurately described his knowledge revealed to him by God of Jesus' true identity? Was it because of the special personal relationship they shared? Or were the revelation and the relationship somehow intricately bound?

For two thousand years, Christians have pondered the ambiguities of this conversation. We have reiterated both Jesus' and Peter's words, and we have elaborated on them in a sometimes bewildering variety of ways. We have named and renamed Jesus himself in an effort to capture the complex meanings of his life: Savior, servant, Lord, brother, friend, "very God of very God." We have built and rebuilt his church in hundreds of different forms. But despite, or perhaps because of, the intimate simplicity and directness with which Jesus and Peter here address each other, Christians on the whole have found it difficult either to answer Jesus' question to Peter with anything like unanimity or to agree on the implications of their dialogue for the church and the life to which it calls individual believers. Nevertheless, it is not entirely inaccurate to suggest that Christians have tended to look at this encounter between Jesus and Peter in one of two ways. They have either emphasized what might be called *propositions*, or they have stressed *relationships*. (Or, to put it differently, they have seen as predominant either *order* or *freedom*.)

Let us look at this a bit more closely. One way to understand the encounter between Jesus and Peter is to focus on the *content* of the question-and-answer sequence between them. For some persons, Jesus' question and Peter's response constitute a first and critical datum in what is sometimes called our "deposited faith." This is the faith that is handed down, the faith that is centered in and structured on propositions, concrete definitions, theological interpretations, belief statements. Many of the conservative Christians we have been discussing (though certainly not all) fall into this category. They are concerned with *belief in the Christ*, and they expect their fellow believers to assent to certain propositions about Christ and Christ's church.

A second way to understand the encounter between Jesus and Peter is to focus on the *context* in which it took place—the interpersonal dynamic between them. For some Christians the real meaning of the faith does not lie in the particular content of Jesus' and Peter's recorded words. Rather it lies somehow, mysteriously, in the totality of the encounter itself. It lies in the dynamic, personal relationship with Jesus, which is beyond words and definitions. Many people in the mainline churches, as well as some charismatics and pentecostals, understand the encounter in this way. They are concerned less with belief in the Christ than with *knowing* and, most important, *following Jesus*. They expect their fellow Christians to live lives of active caring for others, both inside and outside the fellowship of the church.

While such explanations can be helpful in understanding basic differences among Christians, it is impossible to reduce the many divisions within Christendom to a simple distinction between assent to theological propositions on the one hand and emphasis on relationships and people on the other. Nor do conservative and mainline believers fall into neat patterns under these rubrics. Nevertheless, the distinction is helpful, because it points to a historical difficulty that Christians have had in attempting to remain faithful without truncating the full life of both followership and understanding to which Jesus calls them. A brief description of the church in the years immediately after Jesus' death will help make the nature of this dilemma clear.

It is evident that for the earliest Christians, being a Christian, being faithful, had mainly to do with knowing Jesus Christ and not just knowing about him. Christianity itself was an active, experiential faith that found its dynamic center in small, shared communities of people, not in received, "orthodox" traditions and texts. The four written Gospels make this distinction quite clear. In the Gospel tradition, Jesus himself is portrayed as having less concern for what people believe than for how they go about together in the world acting out those beliefs. A helpful illustration of this action ethic is the familiar story of the good Samaritan, in which Jesus neatly translates the feisty lawyer's *content* question—"Who is my neighbor?"—into a people-centered, *action* answer—"Go thou and do likewise!"

This sort of action ethic was appropriate and probably even essential for a small and intimate society of followers. But at the end of the apostolic age, both the church and its environment were changing. For one thing, the church itself did not stay small or parochial; its people began to diversify radically. By A.D. 70 it had spread all the way from Egypt to Italy and across the cities north and east of the Mediterranean. So Christians no longer shared the same space, the same background, or the same experience and understanding of their faith. It could not be expected, for example, that a pagan convert to Christianity would experience or understand the reality of Jesus the same way a lifelong Jew would.

There was another difference, as well. Second and third generation Christians faced changing theological expectations as well as a diversifying fellowship. Their mothers and fathers in the faith had never engaged in long-range planning for their institutional church life, because they had not expected to be around long enough to need it. They believed wholeheartedly in the imminent second coming of Christ, and they were convinced that the final working out of God's cosmic drama was, even in their lifetimes, hurtling toward a climax. But by the end of the first century it was apparent to most Christians that the church was probably in for a longer worldly wait than anyone, including Paul himself, had anticipated.

In these unexpected and extended "between times," now characterized by a dispersed and diversifying fellowship, the preservation and propagation of the faith hinged on more than merely following and waiting. It depended increasingly on saying precisely who it was that believers followed and why, what they actually believed, what their common understandings were supposed to be. And this sort of clear articulation was all the more critical in a world of competing faith claims in which Christianity was only one movement among many (including many Christian counterfeits), each telling and selling its unique story in a busy theological marketplace.

Thus at the close of the apostolic age, the church faced a dilemma that Christians from Paul to Martin Luther to today's mainline and conservative American denominations have faced. It is this: How can a movement that is *essentially* personal, dynamic, interactive, become meaningfully embodied as an institution and so perpetuate itself across the years? Or, to put the question more personally: When individual Christians reflect on the meaning of Jesus' question to each of us, "Who do you say that I am?" how can their answers reflect both the import of Peter's defining response (that is, his proposition about Jesus' nature) and the import of his active followership (his personal relationship with Jesus) that made such a response possible in the first place?

A familiar poem by Robert Frost entitled "The Road Not Taken"[1] describes the dilemma of a traveler in the midst of a journey. "Two roads," says the narrator of the poem, "diverged in a yellow wood." Unable to take them both, the narrator chooses one, the road less traveled, and that, he says, has made "all the difference." The common perception is that Frost's poem is primarily about risk taking and exploration. But, in fact, it is concerned with much more than that. It is about the hard necessity (or from another perspective the luxury) of choice itself, because taking either road would have made "all the difference" to the chooser.

It was the genius of the early church that when faced with the possibility of divergent paths to faithfulness—paths centered on propositions and paths centered on persons—it chose not to choose. Instead, it committed itself to taking both roads. This commitment is evident in the rich biblical imagery handed down to us. In beginning to articulate the nature of their shared faith, Paul and other architects of the New Testament canon provided early Christians with very special descriptive imagery. This imagery, on the one hand, gave their church definition, order, and structure; and, on the other, constantly called it back to its original, people-centered, Spirit-filled, prophetic origins.

What are these special images? The most familiar of them is the church as the body of Christ, which Paul uses in the twelfth chapter of his first letter to the church at Corinth. But there are other arresting images elsewhere in the New Testament: in John, Jesus' description of himself as the vine with branches and fruits; in 1 Peter, the image of Christ as the cornerstone of a spiritual building always under construction; in Revelation, the church in the marriage relationship as Bride of the Lamb.

What these several metaphors have in common is their expression of the unique relationship of Christ and his followers as one of a diversity of people and propositions, beliefs and actions, faith and followership. These alternatives are not presented as antagonistic impulses or choices between opposite paths. Rather they exist—or should exist—in a harmony essential to the very being, function, and vitality of the whole. As metaphors they provide Christians with a warrant for and a basic description of the kind of dynamic, wholistic structures and institutions they might create in order to perpetuate their beliefs and maintain their necessary institutional boundaries. Yet for the individual believer, the full meaning of these metaphors is dependent finally upon his or her own experience of Jesus the Christ. And that experience is not a concept but a personal relationship, a mystery that will be apprehended uniquely and personally by each one who calls Jesus friend and Lord.

What does all this mean for American Christians attempting to live faithful lives today? Perhaps above all, it means that mainline and conservative Christians alike are called to understand themselves wholistically, as a fellowship. They are to hold in creative tension the great, hard disparities that give life and form to the church. For in being the body of Christ, Christians do not, like Robert Frost's traveler, have the luxury of choice. They cannot make the easy and obvious choice to follow only one metaphoric pathway, although many in the church have tried to do so. Their fellowships need to be both/and, not either/or, fellowships, concerned equally about limitations and growth, rules and relationships, order and freedom.

For mainline and conservative Christians today, pursuing both/and fellowships has several specific consequences. First, it means that these groups need to become aware of the tendency of human beings (especially religious ones) to absolutize and universalize their own choices. This is no less true in mainline churches than in conservative ones. For every conservative who has made separation an inviolable first principle of ecclesiology, there is a liberal who has lifted up inclusivity with the same rigid conviction. Second, it means recognizing the partial nature of human knowledge and experience, and the consequent need for a stance of genuine humility in making definitive theological statements. What Paul wrote to the Corinthians is equally important for twentieth-century believers to hear: "Now we see in a mirror dimly, but then face to face. Now I know in part; then I shall understand fully, even as I have been fully understood [1 Cor. 13:12]." For every conservative who is dogmatic about doctrinal specifics, there is a liberal who is dogmatic about not being dogmatic at all. Third, both/and fellowship means recognizing and naming the ways in which each of us habitually erects elaborate intellectual structures to protect ourselves from new possibilities that challenge our treasured certainties. For every conservative who strains to prove that the supernaturally generated scriptures cannot err, there is a liberal who steadfastly refuses to consider the possibility that the supernatural even exists. Last, it means a willingness to approach one another not polemically and judgmentally but dialogically. For every conservative who has rejected serious conversation with mainline Christians on theological grounds, there is a liberal who, also on theological grounds, has lamented the "broken body of Christ" and advocated ecumenical dialogue with everyone *except* those who call themselves conservative.

But this task of dialogue and reconciliation is not easy, and it is complicated by a number of factors. One of these is the voluntary nature of religious bodies in the United States. In its provision that "Congress shall make no law respecting an establishment of religion or prohibiting the free exercise thereof," the First Amendment to the Constitution guarantees that no church or religious group will have legal precedence over another or receive preferential treatment by the government. In actual practice this means that all religious groups, from Moonies to United Methodists, are equal under the law. It also means that all these groups, in effect, must constantly compete with one another for members. It is no accident that mainline and conservative churches alike are concerned with numbers (of churches, dollars, people), for the issue in the United States is one of institutional survival as well as correct theology. Although the First Amendment and the so-called voluntary principle offer priceless safeguards against the possibility of religious intolerance and coercion, they also breed a spirit of competition and antagonism often antithetical to cooperation and wholistic fellowship. Although it is pleasant to imagine that our beliefs and practices are free from the taint of pragmatism, the reality is otherwise. Churches that can persuade people that they have more truth claims, more authenticity, more spiritual power, will likely survive; churches that appear to meet people's needs and desires, whether or not these are godly ones, will likely prosper.

During the better part of this century, a second factor has been the struggle for power between liberal and conservative Christians in America. It is clear that since the late 1960s the balance of power has shifted somewhat. Although conservatives still represent a minority within American Christendom (especially if Roman Catholics are included with mainline Protestants), they have gained sufficient voice and visibility to be a serious threat to the mainline hegemony of nearly seventy years. Today mainline churches are on the defensive, reeling at the loss of thousands of members over the last twenty years.[2] Nevertheless, despite the political gains of a new conservative Christian voting bloc, for the moment the mainline churches retain the balance of power in those places where decisions are made and policy discussed: the legislatures, the courts, and the public media. The result of this ambiguous situation is, not surprisingly, a wariness on both sides of the theological fence; such wariness naturally lends itself more to suspicion and accusation than to cooperation.

A third factor limiting reconciliation is that regional and demographic factors exacerbate the longstanding antagonism between liberals and conservatives. By now it will be clear that both mainline and conservative Christians are to be found in every social stratum and every educational and economic class. Nevertheless, it is true that many mainline Christians are concentrated in the urban coastal areas of the United States and, perhaps especially, in the Northeast and Middle Atlantic areas. It is also true that many conservatives (particularly those that provide the primary constituency for the Evangelical Right) are located in the nonurban South and West. Moreover, historically these groups have often been distinguished by different educational levels and social backgrounds. These essentially nonreligious differences, some of them reaching back as far as the pre-Civil War period, significantly complicate the possibility of dialogue and understanding. Stereotypes of both groups remain current: conservatives are often characterized as uneducated, bigoted Southerners, while mainline Christians may easily be dismissed as Northern secularists who are part of the effete, Eastern power elite.

Last and most important, real and substantive theological differences clearly exist between mainline and conservative Christians, as we have already seen. Yet only occasionally are these discussed seriously on their own terms. Too often the differences are dealt with by shifting to nontheological categories of interpre-

tation (for example, by the suggestion that fundamentalism represents a case of "arrested growth" in an adolescent, conformist stage
of faith developement[3]). Such familiar, reductionist arguments—
and they are common within both liberal and conservative
camps—are little more than polemics in the guise of description
and understanding. But in fact, the most basic differences between
these groups must be examined first in their own integrity as
theological differences, for above all they have to do with our
divergent understandings about religious authority, the Bible,
leadership and followership, Christian living, the nature of God
and humankind, and other categories of belief. These, like any
beliefs, are inevitably shaped by a host of contextual variables. But
a consideration of the context of belief cannot constructively
ignore its content.

The Past and Future of the Church

In reaching toward dialogue and fellowship between conservatives and liberals, it is helpful to realize that radical theological diversity and conflict represent no new phenomenon. Paul
writes about a similar situation in his first letter to the church at
Corinth, which at the beginning of the sixth century A.D. was
hardly operating by anything like cooperation and theological
consensus. It was, in fact, a veritable smorgasbord of conflicting
theological interest groups. Some followed favorite leaders; some
had distinctive ideas about sex and marriage and family life; some
favored spontaneous ecstatic utterances; some preferred the entice-
ments of Gnostic wisdom;[4] some were semireconstructed pagans,
unwilling as yet to give up all the trappings of the old life.
Evidently the Corinthians were a fractious and difficult lot, not
altogether unlike Christians in America today. Paul's response to
their divisiveness, however, was not to wage polemical battles nor
to reduce their theologies to social and psychological data. Rather
he urged them to unity in the name of a higher theological
principle, Christ himself. For, Paul writes in effect, it is of little use
to speak out righteously and rigidly about your particular perspectives when God momentarily may break in and turn your certainties upside down.

Paul's words and the experience of the Corinthians suggest that an honest examination of history itself may provide a useful point of departure for enabling conservative and mainline Christians to know themselves, one another, and the needs of their church better. For the history of Christianity is the record of the church's long struggle to be the wholistic fellowship it is called to be. It is a record of both failure and success; it offers both humility and hope to contemporary believers.

Another verse by Robert Frost provides helpful insight. Always a seeker himself, Frost was well aware of humankind's impossible, frustrating need to know God fully. In this concise couplet, he describes the frustrating uncertainty inherent in all our attempts to understand the divine:

> We dance around in a ring and suppose,
> But the Secret sits in the middle and knows. [5]

In America today there are thousands of Christian bodies, liberal and conservative alike, each behaving as if its "supposings" were truths. [6] History adds to the number. Most of these tread warily around one another, fearful, perhaps, that their fragile certainties will be revealed for the supposings they really are. But this is the irony: the history of the church reveals them anyway. When William Miller persuaded thousands of followers to sell their earthly goods and await the world's last day on October 22, 1844, he was not the first nor the last to have his careful and prayerful calculations exploded by reality. When liberal proponents of a world-renovating Social Gospel envisioned a progressively better world after the turn of the twentieth century, they did not expect to have their plans undercut by the overwhelming facts of human sin and systemic evil manifested in two world wars and an economic depression.

The examination of history will not prevent new generations of Christians from making the mistakes of the past, albeit in altered contexts and circumstances. But the study of our history is a hedge against triumphalism, rigidity, arrogance, and absolutism of both the left and the right. History demands humility. It offers a reminder of our creatureliness, of the limitations of human imagination and intellect, and of the finitude of human perceptions.

But there is another side to Frost's couplet and another side to the study of history. It may be that the Secret sits in the middle while men and women dance around it in the dark. But if church history is in some sense the story of human folly in the search for God and God's ways, it is also the story of our prevailing centeredness. Church history points to the astonishing reality that despite two thousand years of assorted separations, schisms, and sea changes, this mysterious and elusive (but very present) Secret still remains as the center, still has the power to make us dance. Church history thus offers hope for reconciliation and growth, a hedge against despair and disbelief, even as it chastens our alienating certainties.

In particular, the fresh and thoroughgoing examination of church history challenges both mainline and conservative Christians in several ways. First, it dispels the myths and selective readings of the past that bind Christians to reflexive and patterned ways of behaving and relating to one another and to the world. An honest examination of America's own religious history, for example, undercuts the familiar notion, cherished by many conservatives, that America is uniquely a Christian nation. To be sure, Puritan Congregationalists with utopian dreams of a Christian commonwealth founded Massachusetts Bay and extended their vision far beyond its boundaries. But Jews, Roman Catholics, Deists, and immigrants of other faiths early peopled America's shores, so that by the time of the Revolution, it is estimated that only about 15 to 20 percent of the total colonial population were church members. The reality of religious pluralism, not Protestantism, shaped the policies of the new nation most decisively. Mainline Christians, too, are guilty of reading history selectively. Often, for example, they have ignored their own formative roots in the reflective supernaturalism of Puritanism itself, choosing instead to lift up that strand of New England thought that issued in the rational liberalism of the nineteenth century. Or they have ignored their formation in the fervent experiential evangelicalism of the nineteenth century, preferring to stress the social vision and activism of that period. Awareness of the realities of our own past can open us to new theological insights, new possibilities for growth and interaction with Christian relatives we did not know we knew.

Second, a fresh examination of history challenges Christians to explore the difference between the timeless and the time-bound in our ecclesial lives. Whatever else it may do, history assures us that many of the certainties of today are temporary and ephemeral. Acquaintance with the past permits us to ponder more critically our own unexamined assumptions and givens and to judge them against the values and understandings of other generations of believers. Indeed, the more we know of the church's past, the less likely we are to equate the finite wisdom of today with God's timeless truth, and the more likely we are to be genuinely open to seeing God's handiwork in the whole vast and complex richness of other Christian traditions.

Third, the study of church history challenges Christians to embrace neither a static and unyielding understanding of truth that condemns Christianity to anachronistic pronouncements, nor a flaccid relativism that accommodates willingly to every social change. Church history is the record of tradition: the creeds and confessions, the thinkers and theologians that have provided permanence, structure, and stability for the faithful. But church history is also the record of change and challenge, as, in the words of James Russell Lowell's famous antislavery poem, "new occasions" and "new duties" call Christians to new perceptions of reality. Such perceptions are not fads but revelations, the gifts of a God who does indeed "have more light yet to break forth from his holy Word."[7] Like the vine whose sturdy branches periodically shed their leaves in order to prepare for new growth, the church is organic, growth-filled, and changing, even as it is firmly rooted in the medium that gives it nourishment.

It will not be easy for conservative Christians and mainline Christians to reach out to one another. Different theological norms, structures of power, regional divisions, decades of mutual misunderstanding—all these and other factors have in the past hindered basic civility and easy dialogue among us. But the whole history of the Christian church demonstrates that wherever there is theological and institutional isolation and entrenchment, there is a gospel message that is partial, truncated, lifeless. In mutual conversation we can—and must—be our own best and most trenchant critics, enabling both churches and individual believers to live lives of wholeness and balance in the name of Christ, our common center.

Notes

Introduction

1. It should be noted that the rise of conservative Christianity is not exclusively an American phenomenon but is worldwide.
2. Although some commentators have suggested that the term *oldline* or even *sideline* should now be substituted, *mainline* is the more familiar term. Historically, mainline refers to the several "establishment" denominations that dominated religious thought in America in the late nineteenth and early twentieth centuries, e.g., Presbyterians, Lutherans, Congregationalists, Methodists, northern Baptists, Episcopalians, and others who generally embraced liberal thought.

Chapter 1—Who Are the Conservative Christians?

1. George M. Marsden, "Unity and Diversity in the Evangelical Resurgence," *Altered Landscapes: Christianity in America, 1935–85,* ed. David M. Lotz (Grand Rapids: Eerdmans, 1989), 63.
2. Grant Wacker, "Uneasy in Zion: Evangelicals in Postmodern Society," *Evangelicalism and Modern America,* ed. George M. Marsden (Grand Rapids: Eerdmans, 1984), 17–28.
3. *The Book of Worship* (New York: United Church of Christ Office of Church Life and Leadership, 1986), 510–11.
4. It is important to realize that conservatives themselves may not understand these interpretive differences as a function of social, cultural, and historical variables. Instead they see response to doctrinal statements as evidence of a person's status with God, because they believe the unregenerate cannot comprehend God's truth rightly.
5. *Statement of Purpose* (Bethesda, Md.: Westmoreland Congregational United Church of Christ).

6. Some scholars delineate evangelicals more precisely, with categories that emphasize confessionalism, justice and peace, liberation theology, conciliarism and dialogue, and worship. See, for example, Richard Quebedeaux, *The Young Evangelicals: Revolution in Orthodoxy* (New York: Harper & Row, 1974). Until recently it was not uncommon to use the terms *neo-pentecostal* and *charismatic* interchangeably. Both groups, however, shun the former term because of their group's distinct origins, different theological emphases, and practices.

7. Sydney E. Ahlstrom, "From Puritanism to Evangelicalism: A Critical Perspective," *The Evangelicals: What They Believe, Who They Are, Where They Are Changing*, eds. David F. Wells and John D. Woodbridge (Nashville, Abingdon Press, 1974), 269–89.

8. Scholars distinguish between postmillennialists, who believe that a thousand year reign of righteousness will precede Christ's second coming and judgment, and premillennialists, who argue that Christ's coming will precede and initiate the millennium itself. The former belief was commonly held by nineteenth-century Protestants in the major denominations. It was an optimistic understanding that encouraged many to believe that their own charitable and evangelistic activities could help inaugurate the kingdom. Today these same groups tend to be amillennial, ignoring or rejecting altogether the idea of a millennium. Conservatives, however, tend to be premillennialist in their theology.

9. George M. Marsden, *Fundamentalism and American Culture: The Shaping of Twentieth-Century Evangelicalism 1870–1925* (New York & Oxford: Oxford University Press, 1980), 4.

10. Deane William Ferm, *Contemporary American Theologies: A Critical Survey* (New York: Seabury Press, 1981), 1–7.

11. The specific relationship of fundamentalism to both its nineteenth-century roots and to contemporary evangelicalism is a matter of scholarly debate. Two good sources of information are Marsden, *Fundamentalism and American Culture* and *Reforming Fundamentalism: Fuller Seminary and the New Evangelicalism* (Grand Rapids: Eerdmans, 1987).

12. Jerry Falwell, "Foreward," *Fundamentalism Today: What Makes It So Attractive*, ed. Marla J. Selvidge (Elgin, Ill.: Brethren Press, 1984), 7–8.

13. The National Association of Evangelicals, composed of pentecostal, evangelical, and holiness churches and individual members, specifically distinguished itself from the liberal Federal Council of Churches of Christ in America (now the National Council of Churches of Christ in the U.S.A.) and the fundamentalist American Council of Christian Churches, founded by Carl McIntire in 1940. Today the NAE has upward of five million members.

14. The term *Bible believing* is used broadly in the black churches to refer to evangelicals in general, and not only those characterized here as historic evangelicals. See William H. Bentley, "Bible Believers in the Black Churches," *The Evangelicals* (Nashville: Abingdon Press), 108–21.

15. This term refers to the "infilling" or "pouring out" of the Holy Spirit that believers experience after conversion. It is understood variously. Some pentecostal groups consider it a third "work of grace," following conversion and sanctification; others link conversion and sanctification and so conceive Spirit baptism as a "second work."

16. Vinson Synan, "Frank Bartleman and Azusa Street," *Azusa Street* (Plainfield, N.J.: Logos, 1980), xx.
17. Dennis Bennett, *Nine O'Clock in the Morning* (Plainfield, N.J.: Logos, 1970), 203.
18. " 'Restoration' Teachings Divide Charismatics," *Christian Century* (December 7, 1988): 1117–18.

Chapter 2—Religious Authority and the Churches

1. Quoted in John D. Woodbridge et al., *The Gospel in America* (Grand Rapids: Zondervan, 1979), 110.
2. Ibid., 116.
3. David Allan Hubbard, *What We Evangelicals Believe* (Pasadena: Fuller Theological Seminary, 1979), 17–20.
4. A good example of this way of reading the Bible may be found in the writings of evangelical feminist Virginia Ramey Mollenkott, whose assessments of women's issues and homosexuality use the life and teachings of Jesus to critique apparently contradictory passages elsewhere in the scriptures.
5. Carl Michalson, "Authority," *A Handbook of Christian Theology*, eds. Arthur A. Cohen and Marvin Halverson (Nashville: Abingdon Press, 1958), 22–34.
6. Donald G. Bloesch, *The Future of Evangelical Christianity* (Garden City: Doubleday, 1983), 48–54.
7. Richard Hofstadter, *Anti-Intellectualism in American Life* (New York: Random House, 1962), 86–87.
8. John Jefferson Davis, *Foundations of Evangelical Theology* (Grand Rapids: Baker Book House, 1984), 117–18.
9. Ibid., 133.
10. I am indebted to Professor Gabriel Fackre of Andover Newton Theological School for the understanding of "traditioning."
11. George Gallup, Jr., and David Poling, *The Search for America's Faith* (Nashville: Abingdon Press, 1980), 141.
12. There are exceptions. The contemporary Episcopal church, of course, values tradition highly; historically the nineteenth-century Mercersburg movement argued for an organic conception of the church that did not insist on a radical break with the church's pre-Reformation past and tradition.
13. Not all such groups are conservative. The Christian Church (Disciples of Christ), for example, was a nineteenth-century restoration movement that in many ways sought to return to the simplicity of name, belief, and behavior that marked the early church.

Chapter 3—The Individual Believer

1. Timothy L. Smith, *Revivalism and Social Reform: American Protestantism on the Eve of the Civil War* (New York: Harper & Row, 1957).
2. It was a Congregational minister, Horace Bushnell, whose 1847 work *Christian Nurture* became foundational for a view of faith that rejected

revivalism and promoted an organic understanding of the contributions to faith of family, church, and nation.

3. Bill Bright, *The Four Spiritual Laws* (San Bernardino, Calif.: Campus Crusade for Christ, 1965).

4. These four are not an exhaustive list. For further elaboration of the beliefs held by particular groups, see, e.g., Stanley M. Burgess and Gary B. McGee, eds., *Dictionary of Pentecostal and Charismatic Movements* (Grand Rapids: Zondervan, 1988); Arthur C. Piepkorn, *Profiles in Belief: The Religious Bodies of the United States and Canada*, vols. 3 and 4 (San Francisco: Harper & Row, 1979).

5. For discussion of these developments, see Marsden, "Unity and Diversity."

6. James Davison Hunter, *Evangelicalism: The Coming Generation* (Chicago & London: University of Chicago Press, 1987), 50–75.

7. Mark Ellingsen, *The Evangelical Movement: Growth, Impact, Controversy, Dialogue* (Minneapolis: Augsburg, 1988), 248–53, 312–15.

8. For an excellent study of the way in which the separationist impulse functions and is inculcated, see Alan Peshkin, *God's Choice: The Total World of a Fundamentalist Christian School* (Chicago & London: University of Chicago Press, 1986).

9. D. James Kennedy, *Evangelism Explosion* (Wheaton, Ill.: Tyndale House, 1977).

10. Robert Schuller, *Self-Esteem: The New Reformation* (Waco, Tex.: Word Books, 1982), 98–9.

11. *Baptism, Eucharist, and Ministry*, Faith and Order Paper No. 111 (Geneva: World Council of Churches, 1982), 2–7.

12. It is true that in traditions where confirmation follows infant baptism, as well as in traditions favoring believer's baptism, a "decision for the faith" must be made by a mature believer. But this need not be understood as a radical turning away from the depravity of one's former life. On the contrary, it can represent a confirmation of a life that has already been imprinted with Christian values and thought.

13. *Baptism*, 10.

Chapter 4—The Church and Its Work

1. Lesslie Newbigin, *The Household of God* (New York: Friendship Press), 26–122, 1954; Peter Schmiechen, "Theology and the United Church of Christ," *Prism* (Spring 1988): 3–13.

2. Jerry Falwell, ed., with Edward Dobson and Ed Hindson, *The Fundamentalist Phenomenon: The Resurgence of Conservative Christianity* (Garden City, N.Y.: Doubleday, 1981), 220.

3. Ellingsen, *The Evangelical Movement*, 258.

4. Bloesch, *The Future of Evangelical Christianity*, 127.

5. Harold J. Ockenga, "From Fundamentalism, Through New Evangelicalism, to Evangelicalism," *Evangelical Roots*, ed. Kenneth Kantzer (Nashville: Thomas Nelson, 1978), 44.

6. Charles Woodbridge, quoted in Falwell, et al., *Fundamentalist Phenom-enon*, 152.
7. Ibid., 147.
8. Edward Dobson, *In Search of Unity: An Appeal to Fundamentalists and Evangelicals* (Nashville: Thomas Nelson, 1985), 123–25.
9. George W. Dollar, *The Fight for Fundamentalism* (Sarasota, Fla.: privately printed, 1984), 128–39.
10. John L. Kater, Jr., *Christians on the Right: The Moral Majority in Perspective* (New York: Seabury Press, 1982), 110–11.
12. All quotations are from *Baptism, Eucharist, and Ministry*.
13. An important exception is those evangelicals and charismatics in main-line churches, who most often share the sacramental teaching of their denominations.
14. Nevertheless, Paul's words do carry the suggestion that different gifts do have something like graduated values. See 1 Corinthians 12:28–31.
15. Quoted in Sydney E. Ahlstrom, *A Religious History of the American People*, vol. 2 (Garden City: Image Books, 1975), 346.
16. By "cultural imperialism" is meant the implicit or explicit assumption that western or American culture is superior to other cultures and should be inculcated along with Christianity.

Chapter 5—The Church and Society

1. H. Richard Niebuhr, *Christ and Culture* (New York: Harper & Row, 1951), passim.
2. Burgess and McGee, eds., *Dictionary of Pentecostal and Charismatic Movements*, 521–26.
3. These terms are used to suggest not simply conservative Christianity but conservative Christianity that has been "politicized" and that therefore shares significant areas of concern and activity with traditional right-wing politics.
4. Robert T. Handy, *A Christian America: Protestant Hopes and Historical Realities* (New York: Oxford University Press, 1971), 45.
5. David O. Moberg, *The Great Reversal: Evangelism Versus Social Concern* (Philadelphia: J.B. Lippincott, 1972).
6. Robert D. Linder, "The Resurgence of Evangelical Social Concern, 1925–1975," *The Evangelicals*, 220.
7. Carl F. H. Henry, *The Uneasy Conscience of Modern Fundamentalism* (Grand Rapids: Eerdmans, 1947), 68.
8. The Moral Majority was formally dissolved in 1989.
9. Conservatives are critical of the ecumenical movement, especially as represented by the National Council of Churches and the World Council of Churches, for several reasons. First, it represents to them the watering down of doctrinal precision in the name of a false unity. Second, it is concerned primarily with those churches for which doctrines, creeds, and formal tradition are of primary importance, rather than conversion and spiritual renewal. (For those conservative groups who are especially critical of Roman Catholic and Orthodox bodies, this is of even greater

import). Finally, conciliar ecumenism has been associated with support for a variety of left-wing causes and programs for social renewal that have, in the words of Jerry Falwell, "turned a deaf ear to the Gospel in favor of social renewal without Christ" (Falwell, *The Fundamentalist Phenomenon*, 218).

10. As with all descriptive categories, these must be taken with caution, because they tend to imply formal boundaries where none exists. These four categories in no way represent anything like organized groupings but are meant to suggest representative points of view. At the grassroots level, conservatives, like mainline Christians, often avoid social activism in practice, even when in theory they affirm its appropriateness.

11. Although the above categories are my own, I have used material from two other typologies: Ellingsen, *The Evangelical Movement*, 273–84; and Robert K. Johnston, *Evangelicals at an Impasse: Biblical Authority in Practice* (Atlanta: John Knox Press, 1979), 77–112.

12. Grant Wacker, "Searching for Norman Rockwell: Popular Evangelicalism in Contemporary America," *The Evangelical Tradition in America*, ed. Leonard I. Sweet, (Macon: Mercer University Press, 1984), 288–315.

13. Quoted in Peggy L. Shriver, *The Bible Vote: Religion and the New Right* (New York: Pilgrim Press, 1981), 9.

14. Robert N. Bellah, "Civil Religion in America," *American Civil Religion*, eds. Russell E. Richey and Donald G. Jones (New York: Harper & Row, 1974), 25.

15. Mark A. Noll, Nathan O. Hatch, and George M. Marsden, *The Search for Christian America* (Westchester, Ill.: Crossway Books, 1983), 127.

16. Focused concern about "secular humanism" dates approximately to the late 1970s.

17. Tim LaHaye, *The Battle for the Mind* (Old Tappan, N.J.: Revell, 1980), 26, passim.

18. Jerry Falwell, *Listen, America!* (Garden City, N.Y.: Doubleday, 1980), 150.

19. Mainline Christians and others would argue that the family as defined by the Evangelical Right is not "traditional" at all but a European-American model that is only one of many possibilities, and that the Bible does not present a single view of marriage or family. More radical critics suggest that the "traditional" family is in trouble *because* it is a basically dysfunctional model.

20. In view of the political changes in Europe and the Communist bloc countries, it seems inevitable that the perspectives of the Evangelical Right will undergo some shifting during the next few years. Nevertheless, the Right's anti-Communist stance is deep and thoroughgoing, and suspicion of Communist duplicity is not likely to disappear soon, even in the face of concrete democratizing trends.

21. Considering their general neglect of the doctrine of Christ's second coming, mainline Christians have never been overly concerned with detailing the events of the end times. For conservatives, however, these are important matters that merit careful scrutiny; they are also matters about which there is significant controversy. Basically, conservatives

understand the rapture to be God's "catching up" or "catching away" the church to meet Christ in the air at the end of the age (1 Thessalonians 4:15–17). Pretribulationists believe that the church will be raptured *before* the Antichrist appears and the time of tribulation begins; thus Christians will be spared from suffering. Midtribulationists believe that the church will be caught up sometime during the period of trial and so will witness God's initial judging actions against those who have rejected Christ. Posttribulationists expect that Christians must suffer through the reign of Antichrist and the time of trial along with others; they will be caught up only at the time of Christ's second coming. Premillennial dispensationalists are, almost by definition, pretribulationists.

22. Timothy P. Weber, *Living in the Shadow of the Second Coming: American Premillennialism, 1875–1982* (Chicago & London: University of Chicago Press, 1987), 204–26, passim.

Chapter 6—The Whole Body of Christ

1. From *The Poetry of Robert Frost,* edited by Edward Connery Lathem. Copyright 1916, © 1969 by Holt, Rinehart and Winston. Copyright 1942, 1944 by Robert Frost, copyright © 1970 by Lesley Frost Ballantine. Reprinted by permission of Henry Holt and Company, Inc.
2. William Hutchison points out, in an article that warns against the dangers of citing statistics without sufficient comparative data, that this recent loss is less alarming when it is compared to losses experienced by the mainline churches in the 1930s. Similarly, he notes that growth in conservative churches is not new; "conservative churches have been booming since the Scopes trial." See William R. Hutchison, "Past Imperfect: History and the Prospect for Liberalism," *Liberal Protestantism: Realities and Possibilities,* eds. Robert S. Michaelson and Wade Clark Roof (New York: Pilgrim Press, 1986), 65–82.
3. Robert W. Shinn, "Fundamentalism as a Case of Arrested Development," *Fundamentalism Today,* 91–98.
4. Gnosticism was a movement that in a variety of forms challenged the early Christian church. It stressed the acquisition of secret wisdom (or gnosis) as the primary means for religious development.
5. See endnote 1 above.
6. No one knows the exact number of discrete Christian groups, especially if independent local congregations and fellowships are taken into account. For larger and more stable bodies, a standard reference is Arthur C. Piepkorn, *Profiles in Belief,* vols. 1–4 (New York: Harper & Row, 1979).
7. These are the often-repeated words uttered by Pastor John Robinson as he said farewell to the departing Pilgrims in 1620.

Bibliography

Bloesch, Donald G. *The Future of Evangelical Christianity.* Garden City: Doubleday, 1983.

Burgess, Stanley M. and Gary B. McGee, eds. *Dictionary of Pentecostal and Charismatic Movements.* Grand Rapids: Zondervan, 1988.

Ellingsen, Mark. *The Evangelical Movement: Growth, Impact, Controversy, Dialogue.* Minneapolis: Augsburg, 1988.

Marsden, George M. *Fundamentalism and American Culture: The Shaping of Twentieth-Century Evangelicalism, 1870–1925.* New York & Oxford: Oxford University Press, 1980.

———. *Reforming Fundamentalism: Fuller Seminary and the New Evangelicalism.* Grand Rapids: Eerdmans, 1987.

Selvidge, Marla J., ed. *Fundamentalism Today: What Makes It So Attractive?* Elgin, Ill.: Brethren Press, 1984.